NEWTON PAGE

JOHN LAW

The Lauriston Lecture and Collected Writings

selected and edited

By

GAVIN JOHN ADAMS

NEWTON PAGE

NEWTON PAGE

'John Law'

The Lauriston Lecture and Collected Writings

selected and edited

by

Gavin John Adams

First published by Newton Page 2017

1 3 5 7 9 10 8 6 4 2

ISBN 978-1-934619-15-5

Library of Congress Control Number: 2017915030

Printed in the United States of America
Set in Adobe Garamond Pro

CONTENTS

PREFACE

John Law of Lauriston (1671-1729) is one of the most enigmatic and influential figures in modern history. He is also one of the least well known. Outside of the academic disciplines of monetary economics and financial history, he is now almost entirely forgotten. It is surprising that the contributions of a man who was once the most famous, powerful and celebrated figure in Europe are now barely acknowledged, let alone understood. It is particularly surprising because John Law's ideas and deeds have provided the ideological foundations upon which much of our modern world has been constructed.

It was not always so. From the early eighteenth-century when Law's power was at its height, until the beginning of the twentieth century, the public still clamored after stories about the man who Adam Smith disparagingly called 'the famous Mr. Law'.

This book contains a number of less well-known accounts of the life and significance of John Law by some of the greatest writers of that period, including: Voltaire, one of the greatest intellectual figures of the enlightenment, known for the biting satire *Candide* (1759); Adam Smith, the most famous economist of all time, known for the groundbreaking classic *An Inquiry into the Nature and Causes of the Wealth of Nations* (1776); Charles Mackay, the journalist, known for the early study of crowd psychology *Memoirs of Extraordinary Popular Delusions and the Madness of Crowds* (1841); Washington Irving, the essayist and short story writer known for *Rip Van Winkle* (1819) and *The Legend of Sleepy Hollow* (1820); and Bram Stoker, the architect of the infamous gothic horror novel *Dracula* (1897). It also contains a previously unpublished transcription of a modern lecture on the life of John Law that I had the pleasure to deliver at Law's ancestral home of Lauriston Castle in Edinburgh (2011).

The availability of the accounts of the life and significance of John Law contained in this book have predominantly remained the preserve of the few who are privileged enough to have access to the rare book departments of the major public libraries and universities. Against that background, and in keeping with Newton Page's philosophy of liberating such material from needless exclusivity, one of the main objectives in putting together this collection has been to ensure the accounts become, and remain, easily accessible to the wider public for both convenient study and casual reading. This collection is intended to supplement the publication by Newton Page of several other volumes relating to John Law and his Mississippi Scheme.

Gavin John Adams
June 2016

NOTE ON THE TEXT

During the 250-year period in which the accounts of the life and significance of John Law of Lauriston contained in this book were written and published, conventions of spelling, grammar, punctuation, expression, word truncation, vocabulary and general notation underwent considerable change. In addition, the relatively crude publishing standards of the eighteenth and nineteenth centuries were gradually replaced by more exacting standards, which demand both uniformity of typesetting and editorial consistency. As a consequence of those changes, the modern reader is used to a much more polished product than those available at the times when most of these accounts were originally published.

However, notwithstanding the usual expectations of the modern reader, and in full appreciation that the original texts (and their lack of editorial uniformity) are not as easy on the modern eye as they would have been on the eighteenth or nineteenth-century equivalent, the temptation to edit them to conform with modern writing and editing conventions has been resisted. That approach has been taken because to do anything other than retain the original form of the published texts would be to detract from their inelegant and colorful character and, in turn, serve to dilute the coarse strength of both the historical accounts and conclusions they present. For that reason, readers will notice both inconsistent and imaginative forms of spelling throughout certain accounts, consistent with the original text.

There are three minor technical exceptions to the above. First, the archaic long 's', which fell out of favor in the late eighteenth-century, has been removed and replaced with the more familiar and modern short 's'. Secondly, the superfluous italics, endemic in many books of the eighteenth-century have been removed and replaced with a regular text style. Thirdly, a few minor instances of small capitalization have been substituted for regular capitalization.

This collection of writings on the life and significance of John Law of Lauriston has been based on the earliest available publication or manuscript of each of the following:

Adams, Gavin John. 'The Lauriston Lecture: John Law of Lauriston', from the original manuscript of the lecture delivered by Gavin John Adams at Lauriston Castle, Edinburgh, Scotland, 2011.

Stoker, Bram. 'The Mississippi Scheme and its Antecedents', *Famous Imposters*. New York: Sturgis & Walton Company, 1910.

Irving, Washington. 'The Great Mississippi Bubble', *The Knickerbocker: Or, New York Monthly Magazine*, Volume 15. New York: 1840, reprinted in *Chronicles of Wolfert's Roost and Other Papers*. Leipzig: Bernhard Tauchnitz, 1855.

Mackay, Charles. 'The Mississippi Scheme', *Memoirs of Extraordinary Popular Delusions and the Madness of Crowds*. London: Richard Bentley, 1841.

Smith, Adam. 'Of the Nature, Accumulation, and Employment

of Stock', *An Inquiry into the Nature and Causes of the Wealth of Nations,* Vol. II, Chapter II. pp.72-73. London: W. Strahan and T. Cadell, 1776.

Smith, Adam. 'Of the Scheme of Mr. Law', *Lectures on Justice, Police, Revenue and Arms,* Part II: Of Police, Division II, Section 13. Oxford: The Clarendon Press, 1896.

Voltaire. 'Law's System', taken from 'Continuation of the General View of Europe. Regency of the Duke of Orleans. Law's System', *The Works of M. de Voltaire,* Vol.8, Chapter 188. London: J. Newbery, R. Baldwin, W. Johnston, S. Crowder, T. Davies, J. Coote, G. Kearsley, and B. Collins, 1761.

GAVIN JOHN ADAMS

THE LAURISTON LECTURE

'John Law of Lauriston'

delivered at

Lauriston Castle, Edinburgh, 5 December 2011

GAVIN JOHN ADAMS

THE LAURISTON LECTURE

THE LAURISTON LECTURE

JOHN LAW OF LAURISTON

Over two thousand years ago, the Roman poet Quintus Horatius Flaccus – more commonly known today as Horace – elegantly identified that the account of an individual's life can also serve as the account of the lives of others:

Mutato nomine de te fabula narratur [1]

The translation of those words is: change the name and the story is told about you. I open with those words because the account of John Law's life you are about to hear can serve as the account of our lives. John Law's story is also our story. So who was John Law?

John Law has been described in many different ways. The Cambridge economist Alfred Marshall described him as a 'reckless and unbalanced but most fascinating genius';[2] the Harvard economist Joseph Schumpeter described him as '... in a class by himself... in the front ranks of monetary theorists

1. Horace, *Satires*, 1 1. 69-70

2. Alfred Marshall, *Money, Credit and Commerce* (London, 1923), p.41

of all time';[3] and Karl Marx described him as 'the pleasant character mixture of swindler and prophet'.[4]

John Law was born in Edinburgh in April 1671. His mother, Jean Campbell, was the daughter of a successful Ayrshire merchant. His father, William Law, was an eminent goldsmith who became the Deacon of the Goldsmiths of Edinburgh and kept premises to the south of St. Giles near Goldsmith's Hall.

William Law's profession undoubtedly influenced the young John Law. In the late 1600s, goldsmiths were developing business practices that today we would recognize as banking. Merchants would deposit their gold and coins with goldsmiths for safekeeping. In exchange, those goldsmiths would provide those merchants with receipts recording the value of the items they had deposited. Instead of returning to the goldsmiths to redeem those receipts and collect their valuable items for use as payment in their transactions, merchants would instead exchange those receipts with each other as a form of payment. In other words, merchants would use their goldsmith receipts as a form of paper money, the face value of which was backed by the value of the items deposited by the merchant with the goldsmith and for which the goldsmith had issued the receipt – an idea that would later play a significant role in the life of John Law.

By the time John Law was twelve years old, William Law had become so successful that he was able to purchase a country estate. On 4 June 1683 William Law purchased Lauriston Castle. The castle at that time was very different to the sprawling castle you see today. It comprised only the original four-story stone tower house situated on the west of the present structure.

3. Joseph Schumpeter, *History of Economic Analysis* (London, 1954), p.295.

4. Karl Marx, *Das Capital*, Vol. III, Ch.27 (1894), p.441.

But before William Law and his family were able to relocate to Lauriston Castle, his health began to deteriorate. He had been suffering from acute abdominal and back pain and was diagnosed with bladder stones (a prevalent affliction in the seventeenth century). The only possibility of a cure was to undergo a surgical procedure called a lithotomy, or as it was more commonly known, 'the cutting of the stone'. I shall not trouble you with the gruesome details of the procedure, save to say that the 'cutting of the stone' was as horrific and deadly for the patient as it sounds. The mortality rate was high. So high, that Samuel Peyps, the London diarist, who underwent the procedure and survived, celebrated his survival each year on the anniversary of his 'cutting of the stone' as though it were another birthday. William Law traveled to France for his lithotomy but was not as fortunate as Samuel Peyps. Following the operation, he died. He was buried in Scots College in Paris – a city that would later play a significant role in the life of John Law.

In accordance with the terms of William Law's will, the title and income of Lauriston Castle passed to the twelve-year-old John Law.

After his father's death, John Law was sent to boarding school in Eaglesham where he displayed a remarkable aptitude for both mathematics and a discipline named 'manly pursuits' which probably consisted of physically challenging activities such as tennis and fencing.

At the completion of his school education, it seems he had developed into an adventurous and hedonistic character. He did not attend university but instead returned to Edinburgh where he filled his days cultivating his style of dress, satiating his considerable carnal desires, and gambling away his inheritance.

He soon tired of Edinburgh and spied London as a bigger and better playground in which to pursue his sybaritic lifestyle.

That lifestyle inevitably attracted trouble.

By the time John Law was twenty-one years old, he had not only gambled away the cash element of his inheritance, but had also accumulated considerable gambling debts. Unless he could raise money to pay those debts, he faced incarceration in a debtors' prison. The only asset he had was the Lauriston Castle estate, so he asked his mother to sell it on his behalf. She refused. Instead, she used her own well-managed legacy from William Law to purchase Lauriston from John Law, who was then able to use the proceeds of sale to pay off his gambling debts. It was a perfect solution. Lauriston was saved, John Law kept his good reputation, and, for the time being, he avoided being sent to prison. It also marked a turning point in Law's approach to gambling. No longer content to remain a luckless punter at the card table, Law discarded chance and instead set about studying the application of probability theory to gambling. With a mathematical advantage, he soon became very wealthy.

Two years later, on 9 April 1694, Law became embroiled in an event that would fundamentally change the course of his life. According to contemporary accounts, Law had been drinking in the company of a famous man-about-town called Edward 'Beau' Wilson at the Fountain Tavern, located just to the south of the Strand in London, the site of which is now occupied by Simpson's in the Strand. It is not known whether Law and Wilson were in the same place by design or chance, but what is known is that a considerable degree of enmity existed between them, as each had previously written letters to the other full of 'invectives'. An eyewitness claimed that Law and Wilson got into an argument about the contents of those letters. Shortly thereafter, Law left the Fountain Tavern and was followed by Wilson to Bloomsbury Square where they drew swords and fought. According to court records, when they came together:

> Mr. Wilson received a mortal Wound upon the lower part of the Stomach, of the depth of two Inches, of which he instantly died.[5]

Law was arrested and charged with the murder of Wilson. At the Old Bailey, Law claimed that the fight was not a premeditated duel and that he had acted in self-defense when Wilson drew his sword first. The jury rejected Law's claims and found him guilty of murder. He was sentenced to death.

Historians have advanced a number of theories about the real reason John Law killed Edward Wilson. One theory posits that Law was defending the reputation of a woman. Another theory posits that Law was hired as a hitman. The matter remains unresolved.

John Law may have been awaiting execution, but he had friends in high places. Those friends immediately set about trying to save his life. The Earl of Warriston petitioned King William III to pardon Law, but the King refused. The Duke of Shrewsbury also petitioned the King to pardon Law, but again, the King refused. Law's fate seemed sealed; his execution was imminent.

However, just after New Year's Day 1695, a very mysterious thing happened. John Law's prison cell was found empty. By some accounts, the men guarding Law had been drugged, Law's manacles filed, and he was broken out of his cell in the dead of night. By other accounts, Law had walked out of the prison gates after the King unofficially sanctioned his release on the condition it was made to look like an escape. Whatever the actual circumstances were, when Law's absence became public, Edward Wilson's heirs were furious.

A reward was offered in the *London Gazette* for Law's recapture. But strangely, it contained a ridiculously inaccurate

---

5. See: The Proceedings of the Old Bailey, 18 April 1694. Reference Number: t16940418-28.

description of him – one that would more aid than hinder his escape. It may not be beyond coincidence that the *London Gazette* was at that time published under the supervision of the same Duke of Shrewsbury who had petitioned the King to pardon Law.

John Law was officially a fugitive from English justice. Not much is know about the next ten years of his life, but what is known is that he left England and traveled around the financial centers of various European countries where he spent his time making money at the gaming tables. He also spent his time acquiring a significant knowledge of banking, finance, commerce and the economic environments in which each operated. This knowledge, combined with his agile and fertile mind, led Law to produce a number of proposals for the establishment of a land bank as a means of furthering a nation's economic prosperity. He is known to have submitted such proposals to the authorities in England, Scotland, and France, but each was rejected.

In 1705, Law released what was supposed to be an anonymous proposal to the Scottish Parliament for a note-issuing bank. *Money and Trade Considered, With a Proposal for Supplying the Nation with Money* was so much more than a mere proposal for a note-issuing bank. It was a staggeringly original work of genius which not only included proposals for new systems of banking, and the issuing of paper money as a means to stimulate the economy, but also revealed, for the first time, several of the most significant economic concepts ever devised; concepts which would later be espoused by economists such as Adam Smith and John Maynard Keynes without acknowledgement. It was meant for the consideration of the Scottish Parliament, but the ideas it contained fundamentally altered economics, politics, finance, and, consequently, the modern world. John Law's *Money and Trade Considered* is the most influential but least acknowledged work in the history of economics.

Foreshadowing the showmanship and bravado he would later employ in thrusting his economic schemes upon the unsuspecting subjects of Louis XV, Law opened *Money and Trade Considered* in spectacular fashion. In the first paragraph of the first chapter, he nonchalantly tossed the Scottish Parliament what was the most insightful and concise resolution of at least a two thousand year old economic conundrum. The paradox of value poses the question: what gives a particular commodity its value? Or, in other words, why do we afford a non-essential or useless commodity such as a diamond a much greater value than we afford an essential or useful commodity such as water?

Some of the greatest philosophers and economists from at least the time of ancient Greece to the Age of Enlightenment had tried to formulate a comprehensive resolution to the paradox of value, but each had failed. In 380 BCE the classical philosopher Plato argued that the supply of a commodity determined its value. In 1588 the Florentine writer and economist Bernardo Davanzati assert that both the supply of a commodity and the subjective 'vanity of mankind,' determined its value. In the early seventeenth-century, the Italian polymath Galileo Galilei was the first to use the contrasting imagery of water and diamonds to address the paradox. The use of that imagery, however, was the extent of Galileo's contribution to the matter, his assessment being essentially a restatement of Plato's argument that the supply of a commodity determined its value. In 1696 John Locke, the poster-boy of seventeenth-century liberal political philosophy and inaugurator of the eighteenth-century Age of Enlightenment tried to resolve the paradox but produced an incoherent explanation. In order to solve the paradox of value, an inspired breakthrough was required, a quantum leap of economic insight and thought to carry economics to a higher plateau of understanding. That is what John Law delivered.

To solve the paradox of value, Law first separated the concept of value into two elements: (i) value in use, which is how useful something is, and (ii) value in exchange, which is how much something commands in exchange (in either goods or money). Secondly, to solve the paradox, he argued that price is not determined solely by how useful or necessary something is, but by the relative supply and demand for it:

> Goods have a value from the uses they are applied to, and their value is greater or lesser, not so much from their more or less valuable, or necessary uses, as from the greater or lesser quantity of them in proportion to the demand for them.[6]

Law then invoked Galileo's water and diamond imagery to demonstrate the resolution of the paradox:

> For example, water is of great use, yet of little value, because the quantity of water is much greater than the demand for it. Diamonds are of little use, yet of great value, because the demand for diamonds is much greater, than the quantity of them.[7]

John Law's resolution of the paradox of value was original, elegant, simple and groundbreaking. It demonstrated a remarkably sophisticated understanding and application of the concepts of supply, demand and scarcity. It was a beautifully concise invocation of the influence of what we now call market

---

6. John Law, *Money and Trade Considered, With a Proposal for Supplying the Nation with Money* (1705), reprinted in: John Law, *Money and Trade Considered, With a Proposal for Supplying the Nation with Money*, Newton Page (Washington D.C., 2013), p.7.

7. *Ibid*

forces and an explanation of the price mechanism. Law was, both in analysis and expression, way ahead of his time.

But John Law's role in resolving the Water Diamond Paradox has been largely forgotten. The name now associated with it is another Scottish economist, Adam Smith. Writing over seventy years after the publication of *Money and Trade Considered*, Smith's celebrated restatement of the paradox of value, in *An Inquiry into the Nature and Causes of the Wealth of Nations* is astonishing not for its originality, but for its similarity with John Law's resolution decades before:

> The word value, it is to be observed, has two different meanings, and sometimes expresses the utility of some particular object, and sometimes the power of purchasing other goods which the possession of that object conveys. The one may be called "value in use"; the other, "value in exchange." The things which have the greatest value in use have frequently little or no value in exchange; and, on the contrary, those which have the greatest value in exchange have frequently little or no value in use. Nothing is more useful than water: but it will purchase scarce anything; scarce anything can be had in exchange for it. A diamond, on the contrary, has scarce any value in use; but a very great quantity of other goods may frequently be had in exchange for it.[8]

Adam Smith failed to reference John Law's role in the resolution of the paradox of value. For that reason, Smith is now more frequently credited with Law's resolution than Law himself. Although Adam Smith cannot technically be charged with plagiarism, as plagiarism is not the theft of ideas but of words, he is, in respect of his unacknowledged restatement of John Law's resolution of the paradox of value, only a few

8. Adam Smith, *An Inquiry into the Nature and Causes of the Wealth of Nations* (1776), Book One, Chapter 4.

syllables removed from guilt. Sir Issac Newton (who was also well known for failing to acknowledge the contributions of others) remarked in a famous letter to his rival polymath Robert Hooke on 5 February 1676:

> If I have seen a little further it is by standing on the shoulders of Giants.

It is one thing to see further by standing on the shoulders of giants. It is another thing entirely to clamber up a giant's back, enjoy the view, and silently accept praise for being ten feet tall.

If you would like to see evidence of the influence of John Law's resolution of the paradox of value, before Adam Smith restated it, you can even find it in the pages of the early eighteenth-century novel *Robinson Crusoe* written by Daniel Defoe. Crusoe, who is a castaway on a remote island, contemplates that the money and precious metals in his possession which have very little value in use would also have very little value in exchange on his island when compared to scarce foodstuffs, and that a drawer full of diamonds would be valued on the same basis:

> I had, as I hinted before, a parcel of money, as well gold as silver, about thirty-six pounds sterling. Alas! there the sorry, useless stuff lay; I had no more manner of business for it; and often thought with myself that I would have given a handful of it for a gross of tobacco-pipes; or for a hand-mill to grind my corn; nay, I would have given it all for a sixpenny-worth of turnip and carrot seed out of England, or for a handful of peas and beans, and a bottle of ink. As it was, I had not the least advantage by it or benefit from it; but there it lay in a drawer, and grew mouldy with the damp of the cave in the wet seasons; and if I had had the drawer full of diamonds, it had been the same case—they had been of no

> manner of value to me, because of no use.[9]

Daniel Defoe was an early pioneer of economic and financial journalism. He was very familiar with John Law and his work. *Robinson Crusoe* was published at the same time as Defoe was writing extensively about John Law in both pamphlets and the popular news press. It is beyond the scope of this particular lecture, but there are some very interesting parallels between, and intersections of, the lives of John Law and Daniel Defoe. To give just one example, it was the notoriously sadistic and reputedly corrupt English judge Sir Salathiel Lovell who both sentenced John Law to death for killing Edward Wilson and also sentenced Daniel Defoe to be publicly humiliated for days in a pillory and then incarcerated for an indeterminate term of imprisonment for seditious libel, in the expectation that Defoe would remain incarcerated for the rest of his life.

In addition to solving the paradox of value, proposing models of supply and demand, market forces, and the price mechanism, *Money and Trade Considered* advanced several other extremely important contributions to the field of economics.

In relation to the nature of money, Law proposed the view that money need not have any intrinsic value like gold or silver coins, only that it represents value and is a medium of exchange.

> Money is not the value for which goods are exchanged, but the value by which they are exchanged . . . [10]

In other words, it doesn't matter if money is made from clay tablets, shells, gold, paper or modern day electronic numbers. Its significance is not its intrinsic worth but the value it represents.

---

9. Daniel Defoe, *Robinson Crusoe* (1719), Chapter IX - A Boat.

10. John Law, *Money and Trade Considered, With a Proposal for Supplying the Nation with Money*, Newton Page (Washington D.C., 2013), p.92.

It was undoubtedly an idea commensurate with the practice of the merchants Law had seen as a child, exchanging their goldsmiths' receipts as a form of payment. It wasn't necessary to use gold and silver when paper is more efficient, portable and cheap. Unlike precious metals, paper doesn't need to be mined; it is easily created. Money needs only to facilitate exchange, not be intrinsically valuable.

By what is now known as the 'circular flow of income', Law demonstrated that an increase in the money supply could transform an economy from a stagnant barter economy into one capable of supporting a thriving manufacturing sector.

By what is now known as the 'cash-in-advance constraint', Law demonstrated a positive correlation between the supply of money and economic activity and advanced the proposition that it was necessary to introduce money into an economy in order to enable it to grow and thrive.

He advanced the understanding of the interplay between the amount of money in the international economy and the level of domestic inflation by demonstrating how an international increase in the money supply can lead to domestic inflation even when the domestic economy is in recession.

By what is now known as the 'law of one price', Law demonstrated that prices in an open domestic economy are not dictated solely by the activity in that domestic economy but by the supply and demand in the international economies with which that domestic economy trades.

Notwithstanding its groundbreaking content, the Scottish Parliament rejected the proposals contained in *Money and Trade Considered* (more on the basis of Law's murderous past than the intrinsic worth of the proposals).

With the ratification of the Acts of Union (1707) between England and Scotland fast approaching, Law was forced to flee Edinburgh for Continental Europe. As a fugitive from English justice, his safety in Scotland could no longer be guaranteed. Political union meant his prior conviction for murder in England could become actionable in Scotland whereupon he could be arrested and returned to London to be executed.

Law spent the next eleven years wining at the gaming table and modifying his ideas to suit the various authorities in Europe to whom he would present them. Time after time they were rejected, but Law remained undeterred. Convinced of the veracity, viability and suitability of his proposals, he would advocate them to anyone willing to listen. His tenacity soon began to pay both figurative and literal dividends.

In France, the financial cost of the Nine Years' War (1688-1697) and the War of the Spanish Succession (1701-1714), combined with the mismanagement of the public purse, had almost emptied the coffers of Louis XIV. Domestic deflation had all but ended the availability of credit, and economic activity was languishing. The French economy was edging towards collapse.

In 1715, Louis XIV died and the financially progressive Philippe, Duc d'Orléans was made Regent. John Law wasted no time in lobbying him with proposals for the establishment of a revolutionary note-issuing state bank to facilitate the recovery of France's shattered finances. Although his proposals were rejected by the Conseil de Finance, Law's ideas had piqued the curiosity of the Regent who encouraged Law to submit a reformed proposal for a less controversial note-issuing private bank capitalized by shareholders. Law obliged.

On 2 May 1716, Law was granted a charter establishing his private Banque Générale. Eleven years after the publication of *Money and Trade Considered*, and after incessant lobbying of European leaders, he was able, albeit in a very modest fashion, to begin implementing his ideas.

The Banque Générale was no ordinary deposit-taking

bank. It was also an instrument of public policy, designed to implement Law's ideas on how to improve France's finances and stimulate the economy.

It issued its own banknotes backed by deposits of specie, and practiced what is now known as 'fractional reserve banking'. That meant it was able to increase the amount of money in circulation in the economy by issuing approximately 100 livres of banknotes for each 25 livres of specie deposited in the bank's reserves. In other words, it created 75 new livres for each 25 livres deposited. The maintenance of specie reserves close to 25% of banknotes issued was a conservative and prudent measure that ensured the integrity of the bank's credit. Providing no more than 25% in value of the banknotes were redeemed for specie at the same time, it was considered that the bank could meet its obligations to its depositors. As John Law increased the supply of money, that money began to stimulate commerce in the economy.

The Banque Générale benefited greatly from the royal patronage of the Regent. As a result, it became incrementally involved with the state's finances. Its banknotes were deemed legal tender for the payment of state taxes, and it became the unofficial bank of the state treasury. It pioneered new methods of debt restructuring to help improve the state finances. For example, it initiated what is now known as a debt/equity swap, by purchasing state debt from state bondholders in exchange for shares in the Banque Générale.

As initially modest as Law's Banque Générale was, his personal ambition and ideas remained decidedly immodest.

Law was an opportunist who was always looking to impress, and increase his standing with, the Regent. In June 1717, an opportunity arose for Law to broker the purchase of one of the most beautiful and famous diamonds in history: The Pitt Diamond. The Pitt Diamond had a gruesome history. It was originally 410 carats in its uncut form, which is about the size of a golf ball. A slave in a Golconda mine in south India found it, and stole it by pushing it into an open wound in his leg to conceal it. He tried to sell it to an English captain who considered the life of the slave the best price so killed him and took it. That captain then sold it to a merchant who in turn sold it to Thomas Pitt, the Governor of Madras in India and ancestor of the William Pitt Prime Ministers. Pitt sent it to London where it took two years to cut into a 141-carat cushion brilliant stone. Law convinced the Regent that, despite France's dire financial predicament, the acquisition of the diamond would ultimately be to his eternal glory. The Regent was persuaded and purchased it for the equivalent of $30 million US dollars. Today, however, it would be priceless. The Regent modestly renamed it 'The Regent'. It subsequently adorned the crowns of Louis XV and Louis XVI. It was worn by Marie Antoinette, and then embellished the sword of Napoleon Bonaparte. The Regent Diamond is now displayed in the French royal treasury in The Louvre as one of the museums greatest treasures. Although, Law was correct in his assessment that the Regent Diamond would become a symbol of royal glory. It would later become a symbol of the wastefulness and extravagance that ultimately led to the undoing of the French monarchy.

Almost immediately after Law brokered the acquisition of the diamond to bring glory to the Regent, the Regent decided to return the favour to bring glory to Law.

While lobbying the Regent for permission to establish a bank, Law had written him a cryptic but enticing letter expressing his intention to unleash a scheme that would revolutionize the fortunes of France:

But the bank is not the only nor the greatest of my ideas. I will

> produce a work that will surprise Europe by the changes it will bring in France's favour, greater changes than those brought by the discovery of the Indies or by the introduction of credit. By this work Your Royal Highness will be in a position to relieve the kingdom of the sad position into which it has fallen, and to make it more powerful than it has ever been, to establish order in finances, to replace, support and increase agriculture, manufacturing and commerce, to increase the population and the revenues of the kingdom, to reimburse useless and onerous charges, to increase the revenues of the King while helping the people, and to reduce the state debt without doing wrong to the creditors . . . [11]

If establishing the Banque Générale had been the first step in Law's revolutionary scheme, establishing a trading company would be the next.

In August 1717, Law was granted permission to establish the Compagnie d'Occident. Just like the Banque Générale, it also served to assist the treasury by being initially capitalized by government debt in return for shares. It would raise more capital by offering series of attractive share issues to investors. That capital was to be used for financing its acquisitions, raising working capital to fund its trading operations, paying dividends due to existing shareholders, and even taking control of the entire French national debt.

The Compagnie d'Occident acquired exclusive trading rights to the whole of French Louisiana, Asia and Africa, and the rights to the quasi-public functions of operating the royal mints and gathering state taxes. It was renamed the Compagnie des Indes, but is more commonly known today as the Mississippi Company. It was a gargantuan organization.

With a monopoly over trading and tax-gathering rights, a

---

11. Letter from John Law to the Regent, cited in: Janet Gleeson, *The Moneymaker* (London, 1999), p.107.

stranglehold over certain quasi-public functions, optimistic pronouncements regarding its operational prospects, and promises of enviable dividends for investors, the public's interest in acquiring the shares of the Mississippi Company began to increase.

But in order for the public to purchase Mississippi Company shares, they needed access to money. That money became available when John Law's Banque Générale was nationalized by the Regent and became the Banque Royale.

The Regent retained Law as the head of the Banque Royale, but his former bank's restrictive practice of maintaining specie reserves of close to 25% of issued banknotes was discarded. The number of banknotes the new bank could print and issue to the public was now practically unlimited, and it set about printing money to stimulate economic activity. It was a reflationary tactic taken directly from the pages of Law's *Money and Trade Considered*. It didn't disappoint. With each increase in the supply of money in the economy, economic activity soared.

John Law was now at the helm of both the Mississippi Company and the Banque Royale. It was a scarifying and powerful combination. The shares in his Mississippi Company were in high demand, and his Banque Royale was printing the money that enabled the public to purchase them. That was the Mississippi Scheme.

Paris was gripped with frenzied speculation in the shares of the Mississippi Company. With each new positive Mississippi Company trading announcement, each new issue of Mississippi Company shares, and each rise in the Mississippi Company share price, prospective Mississippi Company shareholders became increasingly desperate to acquire more Mississippi Company shares. With each increase in the money supply and available credit from the Banque Royale, and with speculative money pouring into Paris from all over Europe, prospective Mississippi

Company shareholders had the ability to finance the purchase of Mississippi Company shares. Against the background of those increases in both the demand for Mississippi Company shares and the availability of finance for their purchase, the price of the Mississippi Company shares rose massively.

Shares that sold for 500 livres only a few weeks earlier were now exchanging hands for 4,000 livres. The price of Mississippi Company shares rose hour-to-hour. Nothing like it had ever been seen before. Paris was witnessing financial history. It was in the middle of the world's first stock market bubble. John Law's Mississippi Scheme had arrived.

Speculators crammed into the filthy Rue Quincampoix for a chance to buy and sell shares in the Mississippi Company. Incredible stories (both real and apocryphal) of the vast fortunes acquired by ordinary people speculating in the shares in the Mississippi Company filled the columns of newspapers and pamphlets.

There was an account of a footman who became so wealthy, that upon taking delivery of his own carriage, he forgot his newly elevated status and instinctively ascended the back of it to drive rather than to the middle of it to be driven. John Law's own coachman resigned after making a fortune, but not before hiring two other coachmen – one for himself and one for Law. There were stories of servants who became personally rich by selling their masters' Mississippi Company shares at higher prices than that required by their masters, and reinvesting the differences between the expected and achieved prices on their own accounts. One such servant made two million livres in three days by reinvesting such differences. Save to say, he did not remain a servant for long. There were instances of children of common parents who became wealthy speculating in Mississippi Company shares being betrothed in marriage to aristocrats by their parents in return for payments to the aristocrats until such children reached adulthood. An enterprising hunchback earned hundreds of thousands of livres by renting out his hump in the Rue Quincampoix to buyers and sellers of Mississippi Company shares who needed a surface upon which to execute their contracts of exchange.

The prospect of acquiring wealth only increased both the demand for and price of the shares. And the higher the share price rose, the more people wanted to buy them. The opportunity seemed too good to pass by. By December of 1719, demand for the shares had pushed the price up to over 10,000 livres. Daniel Defoe described the vast amount of money being issued by the Banque Royale and being exchanged in Paris for Mississippi Company shares as flowing 'like the waters of the Seine'.[12]

The Mississippi Scheme had secured the apparent financial prosperity of France. The economy was awash with money, and the state had been absolved of its crippling national debt.

John Law had become a celebrated figure across Europe. At the end of 1719, as a reward for all he had done for France, Law was appointed Controller-General of Finances. He had become in substance, if not title, the Prime Minister of France. Upon his appointment, the shares in the Mississippi Company reached their apex of 10,100 livres. Foreign governments showered the architect of the economic miracle with accolades. Even Edinburgh gave its exiled son the freedom of the city.

If one were to take a snapshot of Law's status at that moment in history, it would look like this:

> He was: the richest and most powerful non-monarch Europe had ever seen; the Finance Minister of France, and, in all but title,

---

12. See: 'Bubble Mania in France', Mist's Journal, 12 September 1719, reprinted in: Daniel Defoe, *John Law and the Mississippi Scheme: An Anthology*, Newton Page (Washington, D.C., 2014), p.76.

the Prime Minister; the head of France's state bank, the Banque Royale; the head of the Mississippi Company, and as such: had a monopoly on the importation and sale of tobacco; operated all of the twenty-six domestic French mints which produced silver and gold coins; had a monopoly on all French trade with Africa, Asia and Far East; had control over the collection of all of France's indirect taxes; had control over the entire French national debt; had a monopoly on the fur trade with Canada; possessed the entire landmass of what was then Louisiana, which is over 25% of what is now the United States.

He personally owned: the Mazarin Palace (now the Bibliothèque nationale de France, or the National Library of France building in Paris); more than twelve French country estates; several properties in Scotland; several plantations in Louisiana; more than a third of the buildings surrounding the present Place Vendôme in Paris; at least 100 million livres of stock in the Mississippi Company; the Abbé John-Paul Bignon's library of over 45,000 books; and a collection of over 488 paintings, which may have included works by masters such as: Titian, Raphael, Tintoretto, Veronese, Paolo, Holbein, Poussin, Michaelangelo and Leonardo da Vinci.

Put simply, this one-time Scottish gambler and murderer had burst through the ranks of European society to become one of the richest and most powerful men the world had ever seen. It couldn't get any better. It didn't.

Like all financial schemes, the Mississippi Scheme was constructed upon the volatile foundation of confidence. For the public to continue to use the Banque Royale's banknotes, it had to remain confident that those banknotes would retain and represent their stated face value. And for the public to continue to invest in Mississippi Company shares, it had to remain confident that the prospects of the Mississippi Company justified the market price of the shares. Confidence, after all, is merely a state of mind and, as Law was about to discover, minds can change very quickly.

Concerns were being raised about the financial methods behind the economic madness.

There were concerns about the Banque Royale. Questions were being asked about the Banque Royale's relatively small deposits of gold and silver compared with the vast amounts of paper money it had printed and issued to the public. The increase in the money supply had stimulated the economy but what was behind those banknotes? The banknotes had been accepted as a currency by a public reassured by the promise on the face of those notes that, if requested, the bank would pay the bearer the value of the note in specie. But, with many more banknotes issued than specie deposits available, the bank could no longer be able to keep that promise for all banknote holders. The public soon realized that if they failed to get their specie while the bank still had reserves, they might not get any at all. The scene was set for a run on the Banque Royale.

There were concerns about the Mississippi Company. Questions were being asked about the true nature of the Mississippi Company's prospects. Investors had poured money into it reassured by Law's positive assurances about the trading prospects and future profitability of the company. But what, other than his words, were behind those assurances? Rumors began to circulate, by those who had returned from French Louisiana, that the colonial and business prospects there were nothing like as encouraging as Law had claimed. If those rumors were true, the Mississippi Company was overvalued. Shareholders soon realized that if they failed to sell their shares while the price was still high, they might not even be able to recoup what they paid for them. The scene was set for a huge sell-off of Mississippi Company shares and a collapse in the share price.

Anticipating the Mississippi Scheme's collapse, Banque Royale banknote holders began to convert their Banque Royale banknotes into specie (and export that specie to safety), and Mississippi Company shareholders began to sell their shares in the Mississippi Company. Merchants started to refuse to accept the Banque Royale's banknotes as payment. With both Banque Royale banknotes and Mississippi Company shares viewed as toxic, the price of Mississippi Company shares began to plummet.

Propagandist pamphlets such as Daniel Defoe's *The Chimera, or, The French Way of Paying National Debts Laid Open* were exacerbating the public's concerns. Such pamphlets created further uncertainty among Banque Royale banknote holders and Mississippi Company investors by predicting the imminent collapse of the Mississippi Scheme:

> . . . since there is no Foundation equal to the Structure that now stands upon it. . . it must fall at last, and all I can say of it at present can be only this, that when it comes Great will be the fall of it.[13]

John Law was livid. Each piece of anti-Mississippi Scheme propaganda further eroded the confidence of the public and brought the Mississippi Scheme closer to collapse. He tried to counter the negative effects of those tracts by issuing his own propagandist pamphlets which put a much more positive spin

13. Daniel Defoe, *The Chimera, or, The French Way of Paying National Debts Laid Open* (1720), reprinted in: Daniel Defoe, *John Law and the Mississippi Scheme: An Anthology*, Newton Page (Washington, D.C., 2014), p.43.

on the Mississippi Company's future prospects.[14] Unfortunately for Law, after successfully employing propaganda to build the reputation of the Mississippi Company, it no longer had the effect he desired. He also attempted to stop the sell off of Mississippi Company shares by guaranteeing a minimum price of 9,000 livres per share, but even that didn't work.

No longer able to sustain the Mississippi Scheme by controlling the minds of the public, Law set about attempting to control their actions. He implemented a series of deeply unpopular policies designed to keep the public locked into the Scheme.

What followed was a bizarre game of cat and mouse between Law and the public. As investors were exporting their specie to safety, Law banned the export of coins and bullion. In response, investors put their wealth in jewelry. Law then banned the purchase and display of jewelry. In response, investors put their wealth in objects made of gold and silver. Law then banned the production and sale of objects made of gold and silver. In response, investors put their wealth in precious religious artifacts. And so it continued. It would have been comical had it not been so indicative of the panic felt by investors desperate to avoid ruin.

Next, Law attempted to force the public to patronize the Mississippi Scheme by mandating the usage of his Banque Royale banknotes. It became illegal to possess more than 500 livres in value of specie. Any excess over 500 livres had to be redeemed for Banque Royale banknotes. It also became illegal for payments of over 100 livres to be made in anything other than Banque Royale banknotes.

Members of the public were encouraged to turn against

---

14. See: John Law, *The Present State of the French Revenues and Trade, and of the Controversy betwixt the Parliament of Paris, and Mr. Law* (1720), reprinted: Newton Page (Washington D.C., 2015)

each other as financial rewards were offered to those reporting anyone flouting the edicts. A climate of fear, suspicion and revenge descended as the opportunists sought to line their pockets with the misery of their neighbors, and the vengeful sought to vicariously settle old scores via the agents of fiscal enforcement.

John Law became an object of vilification as the nation's collective view of him swung from one of abject adoration to one of absolute abhorrence.

The level of crime began to rise in the capital. Theft, murders and robberies all increased and offenders were regularly executed in public by being broken on the wheel to discourage others. It didn't work.

It was only a matter of time before the public's hatred of Law escalated into violence. On 21 May 1720 he issued a new edict directing that the Mississippi Company share price was to be reduced from 9,000 livres to 5,000 livres and all Banque Royale banknotes were to be devalued by 50%. In theory, it was a sensible attempt to reduce the money supply, but in practice it was an incendiary mistake that only increased already inflamed passions. Civil disobedience and rioting erupted in the streets of Paris as baying mobs directed their fury towards the vestiges of Law's retched Scheme. Angry crowds, reacting against what they considered to be Law once again abusing their trust by stealing half of their remaining wealth, amassed outside the Banque Royale and pelted it with stones. Law's family also came under threat. The nation's patience with Law had come to an end.

Parlement petitioned the Regent to revoke the edict. Law was denounced as corrupt and calls were made for his arrest and execution. He was summoned by the Conseil de Finance to account for the public's reaction to the edict. He arrived to discover his former loyal political allies had now turned and were willing to berate him for his actions. The public was against him, the Parlement was against him, the Conseil de Finance was against him, his former political allies were against him, and now the Regent went against him. Fearing a wider public revolt, the Regent agreed to revoke the edict. It seemed Law's career in France was over.

Law tendered his resignation to the Regent who instead dismissed him and placed him under house arrest for his own safety. Isolated and humiliated, his next destination seemed likely to be the Bastille.

After his dismissal, however, Law continued to work to save the French economy from the implosion of his own Mississippi Scheme. The task was destined to fail. The public's distrust of Law and his Mississippi Scheme continued and the Banque Royale's unpopular banknotes were finally withdrawn. On 27 November 1720, the Banque Royale was closed. The long-suffering Mississippi Company shareholders sought to rid themselves of their floundering shares, which had become more of a liability than an asset. There was nothing more John Law could do. His Mississippi Scheme was at an end. All that remained to be decided was his personal fate.

Constantly abused and harangued whenever in public, and with ill-intentioned gangs ominously monitoring his every move, Law became a prisoner in his own home. Officials repeated calls for the Regent to send him to the Bastille and then have him executed. Public sentiment deemed the Bastille element of that chronology superfluous. A long overdue appointment with eternity seemed to be drawing nearer by the day. Justifiably fearing for his life, he sought and received the Regent's permission to leave France. On 17 December 1720 he fled to Brussels. By January, he was in Venice. He would never set foot in France again. He was financially ruined. He had been forced to leave France with very little, and his assets had been seized by the state while it undertook to assess his personal financial liabilities. Creditors from across Europe pursued him to settle debts, and politically motivated accusations of financial impropriety continued to emanate from France. His only means of income were loans from the few friends who remained loyal to him and his winnings from gambling at the card tables at the Ridotto. It was a frustratingly meager existence for a man with such drive, energy, ambition and ability. He did attempt to return to the centers of European power but nothing came of it. After a short spell in London, where he finally received his formal pardon for the murder of Edward Wilson all those years before, he spent the rest of his life at the gambling tables in Venice, writing long letters of self-justification to his associates, and explaining the viability of his schemes to anyone who would listen.

John Law's life and his Mississippi Scheme had followed an identical arc of trajectory. Law had been both the maker and breaker of the Mississippi Scheme just as the Mississippi Scheme had been both the maker and breaker of Law. His dazzling rise to power had been followed by an equally dazzling fall. It had been a remarkable story. He died in relative poverty on 21 March 1729. He was 57 years old.

In concluding, we can return to our original question: so who was John Law? There are many headline-grabbing descriptions to choose from: gambler, philanderer, duelist, murderer, absconder, and the first 'millionaire'. Each of those descriptions foreshadows a great tabloid story, but each misses the true significance of his life. There have been many gamblers, philanderers, duelists, murderers, absconders and millionaires who have been lost to history. Many we have never heard of. If John Law's significance were to be found only in those headlines, we would not be talking about him today.

I started this lecture with a quotation from Horace because

in many ways the account of John Law's life can also serve as the account of our lives. John Law's story is also our story. How is that so? John Law provided us with a legacy that continues to have a profound impact in the spheres of economics, public policy, finance, and, as a result, the very foundations upon which modern society has been constructed. He has, as a consequence, had a real, lasting and profound practical effect on all of our lives.

Whenever we read or hear about the academic discipline of economics, we are reminded of the legacy of John Law. John Law was a first rate economist. His Money and Trade Considered was a tremendous academic achievement that has formed the (unacknowledged) basis of many of the advancements in our understanding of the economic environment in which we all live. That academic legacy alone would have been enough to secure an exalted place in history, but Law left us with much more than that.

Whenever we hear or read of the modern economic policies of our elected officials, we are reminded of the legacy of John Law. Every time the politicians we elect attempt to increase our standard of living or employment prospects by increasing government spending to stimulate economic activity ('Keynesian economics' as it is called); and every time a national bank tries to increase our standard of living or employment prospects by stimulating economic activity by increasing the money supply ('quantitative easing' as it is called), each of those actions has its ideological origins in the ideas contained in John Law's *Money and Trade Considered*, and the actions of John Law's Mississippi Scheme. Every single developed society in the world has accepted those ideas. Modern society could not, and would not, function in the same way without the acceptance of those ideas.

Whenever we consider the way we build our modern

infrastructure and provide modern public services: our bridges, roads, airports, railways, schools, prisons, and hospitals, we are reminded of the legacy of John Law. Much of that infrastructure is built and provided by public-private partnerships, each of which has its ideological origins in the quasi-public functions of John Law's Mississippi Company.

Whenever we consider the modern companies we rely on for our jobs, goods, and services, we are reminded of the legacy of John Law. The financial instruments such as debt/equity swaps, share issues and rights issues utilized by those companies to improve their finances and raise the money that enables them to both fund and supply those jobs, goods, and services have their origins in the financial techniques pioneered by John Law's Banque Royale and Mississippi Company.

Whenever we, or our pension funds, invest our savings or pension pots in the stock market, we are reminded of the legacy of John Law. The modern rules of public disclosure and financial integrity for companies listed on public stock markets, which aim to protect the hard earned cash we invest in them, have their origins in the economic devastation caused by John Law's Mississippi Scheme.

Whenever we look in our wallets or purses or at our bank accounts, we are reminded of the legacy of John Law. Every time you use a banknote; every time you use a modern coin; every time you use a credit card or debit card; every time you use internet banking; every time you use any modern crypto currency; every time you use a gift voucher; every time you use a poker chip; in fact, every time you enter into any form of transaction that does not rely on bartering, each such transaction has its ideological origins in John Law's idea that money need have no intrinsic value. Your willingness to use those mediums of exchange is your acceptance of that idea. Every single developed society in the world has accepted that idea. Modern society could not, and would not, function in the same way without the acceptance of that idea. In fact, on the 300th anniversary of John Law's birth (almost to the day) John Law's ideas on the nature of money were finally vindicated when the United States untied the value of the dollar from the price of gold. The world has not merely vindicated John Law and his ideas about the nature of money it has fully embraced those ideas.

For each of the foregoing reasons, and there are many more, the life of one man has continued to have a huge impact on all of our lives and our stories; in ways beyond which many of us have ever even imagined. That life was the life of John Law of Lauriston.

BRAM STOKER

THE MISSISSIPPI SCHEME AND ITS ANTECEDENTS

from

Famous Imposters

(1910)

BRAM STOKER

THE MISSISSIPPI SCHEME AND ITS ANTECEDENTS

THE MISSISSIPPI SCHEME AND ITS ANTECEDENTS

The great "Mississippi Scheme" which wrought havoc on the French in 1720 is the central and turning point in the history of John Law, late of Lauriston, Controller General of Finance in France. His father, William Law (grand nephew of James Law, Archbishop of Glasgow) was a goldsmith in that city.

As in the seventeenth century the goldsmiths were also the bankers and moneylenders of the community, a successful goldsmith might be looked on as on the highroad to great fortune. To William Law in 1671 was born his first son John, who had considerable natural talent in the way of mathematics—and a nature which was such as to nullify their use. As a youth he showed proficiency in arithmetic and algebra, but as he was also in those early days riotous and dissipated, we may fairly come to the conclusion that he did not use his natural powers to their best advantage. He was already a gambler of a marked kind. Before he was of age he was already in debt and was squandering his patrimony. He sold the estate of Lauriston which his thrifty father had acquired, and gave himself over to a life of so-called pleasure. His mother, who had family ambitions, bought the estate so that it might remain in the family of its new possessors. He removed himself to London where within a couple of years he was sentenced to death for murder—not a vulgar premeditated murder for gain, but the unhappy result of a duel wherein he had killed his opponent, a boon companion, one Austin who had acquired the soubriquet of "Beau" Austin. Through social influence the death penalty was commuted for imprisonment, and the crime only regarded as manslaughter. He had however to deal with the relatives of the dead man who were naturally vindictive. One of them entered an appeal against the commutation of the sentence. Law, with the characteristic prudence of his time and nationality, did not wait for the leisurely settlement of the legal process, but escaped to the continent where he remained for some years sojourning in various places. Being naturally clever and daring he seems to have generally fallen on his feet. Whilst in Holland he became secretary to an important official in the diplomatic world, from which service he drifted into an employment with the Bank of Amsterdam. Here the natural bent of his mind found expression. Banking in some of its forms is gambling, and as he was both banker and gambler—one by inherited tendency and the other by personal disposition—he began to find his vogue, addressing himself seriously to the intricacies and possibilities of the profession of banking. He was back in Scotland in 1701 (a risky venture on his part for his felony had not been "purged") and published a pamphlet, "*Proposals and Reasons for Constituting a Council of Trade in Scotland.*" This he followed up after some years, with another pamphlet, "*Money and Trade Considered, with a Proposal for Supplying the Nation with Money*"; and in the same year (1709) he pro-pounded to the Scotch Parliament a scheme for a State Bank on the security of land—a venture which on being tried speedily collapsed. This, like other schemes of that period, was based on the issue and use of paper money.

In the meantime, and for five or six years afterwards, he was travelling variously throughout Europe, occupying himself with formulating successive schemes of finance, and in gambling—a process in which he, being both skilled and lucky, amassed a sum of over a hundred thousand pounds. He had varying fortunes, however, and was expelled from several cities. He was not without believers in his powers. Amongst them was the Earl of Stair, then Ambassador to France, who allured by his specious methods of finance, suggested to the Earl of Stanhope that he might be useful in devising a scheme for paying off the British National Debt. After the death of Louis XIV, in 1715, he suggested to the Duke of Orleans, the Regent for the young King (Louis XV), the formation of a State Bank. The Regent favoured the idea, but his advisers were against it; it was, however, agreed that Law might found a bank with power to issue notes and accept deposits. This was done by Letters Patent and the Banque Générale came into existence in 1710, and was an immediate success. Its principle was to issue paper money which was to be repayable by coin. Its paper rose to a premium in 1716; in 1717 there was a decree that it was to be accepted in the payment of taxes. This created a new form of cheap money, with the result that there was a great and sudden extension of industry and trade. From this rose the idea of a new enterprise—The Mississippi Company—which was to outvie the success of the East India Company incorporated by Charter in 1600 under the title of "The Governor and Company of the Merchants of London trading to the East Indies," which after periods of doubtful fortune, and having become consolidated with its rival "The General East India Company;"—partially in 1702, and completely in 1708, under the somewhat elephantine name of "The United Company of Merchants of England trading to the East Indies"—was now a vast organization of national importance. To the new French Company for exploiting the Mississippi Valley was made over Louisiana (which then included what were afterwards the

States of Ohio and Missouri). The Decree of Incorporation was issued in 1717. The Parliament at Paris presently grew jealous of such a concession having been given to a foreigner; and the next year a rumour went about that Parliament was about to have him arrested, tried, and hanged. The Regent met the parliamentary resistance by making (1718) the Banque Générale into the Banque Royale—the King guaranteeing the notes. Law was made Director General; but he was unable to prevent the Regent from increasing the issue of paper money, by which means he managed to satisfy dishonestly his own extravagance. It was a fiscal principle of the time that the State accountants did not go behind the King's receipt—the acquit de comptant as it was called.

The Western Company was enlarged in 1718 by a grant of a monopoly of tobacco, and of the rights of trading ships and merchandise of the Company of Senegal. In 1719, the Banque Royale absorbed the rights of the East India and China Companies, and then assumed the all-embracing title of Compagnie des Indes. The next year it took in the African Company; and so through that the whole of the non-European trade of France. In 1719, the management of the Mint was handed over to Law's Company; and he was thus enabled to manipulate the coinage. In the same year he had undertaken to pay off the French National Debt, and so become the sole creditor of the Nation. He already exercised the functions of Receiver General and had revenue-farming abolished in its favour. He now controlled the collection and disposal of the whole of the State taxation. At this stage of his adventure, Law seemed a good fiscal administrator. He repealed or reduced pressing taxes on useful commodities, and reduced the price of necessaries by forty per cent, so that the peasants could increase the value of their holdings and their crops without fear of coming later into the remorseless grip of the tax-farmer under the infamous metayer system. Free-trade was in the Provinces practically established. This, so far as it went, was all Law's doing. Turgot, who later got credit for what had been done, only carried out what the Scotch financier had planned.

Law had promised high dividends to the speculators in his scheme, and had so far paid them; so it was no wonder that "The System" raised its head again. In 1719-20, all France seemed to flock to Paris to such a degree and with such unanimity of purpose, that it was difficult to obtain room to go on with the necessary work of the Mississippi Scheme. In such matters, resting on human greed which throws all prudence to the winds, the pressure is always towards the centre; and the narrow street of Quincampoix became a seething mass, day and night, of speculators in a hurry to buy shares. The time for trying to sell them had not yet arrived.

Naturally such a locality rose in value, and as demand emphasises paucity of space, extraordinary prices ruled. Even a small share in the lucky street, where fortunes could be made in an hour, rose to fabulous value. Houses formerly letting for forty pounds a year now fetched eight hundred pounds per month. And no wonder, when shares of the face value of five hundred livres sold for ten thousand! When there is such an overwhelming desire to buy, then is the opportunity for sellers to realise, and the time for such speculation on the one side, and for such commerce on the other, is naturally short and the need pressing.

At the beginning of 1720 everything seemed to be increasing in a sort of geometric ratio. After a dividend of forty per cent, had been declared, shares of five hundred value rose to eighteen thousand. Greed, and the opportunity for satisfying its craving, turned the heads of ordinarily sensible people. The whole world seemed mad. It appeared right enough that the financial wonder-worker who had created such a state of things should be loaded with additional honours. It was only scriptural that he who had already multiplied his talents should be entrusted with more. There was universal rejoicing when John Law—exiled foreigner and condemned murderer—was appointed, in January, 1720, Controller-General of the whole finances of France. Naturally enough, even the hard head of the canny Scot began to manifest symptoms of giving way in the shape of becoming exalté. And naturally enough his enemies—financial, political and racial—did not lose the opportunities afforded them of taking advantage of it. Tongues began to wag, and all sorts of rumours, some of them reconcilable with common sense and easily credible, others outrageous, began to go about. Lord Stair reported that Law had boasted that he would raise France on the ruins of England and Holland, to a greater height than she had ever reached; that he could crush the East India Company and even destroy British trade and credit when he chose. Stair resented this, and he and Law from being close friends became enemies. To appease the incensed and at present all-powerful Law, the powers that were recalled Lord Stair.

On 23 February 1720, the Compagnie des Indes and the Banque Royale were united, thus linking the ends of the financial chain. "The System" was now complete.

When Aladdin set the Genius, who had hitherto worked so willingly, the final task of hanging a roc's egg in the centre of the newly-created palace, he brought the whole structure tumbling about his ears. So it was with John Law and the egregious Mississippi Scheme. His idea was complete and perfect. But the high sun when it reaches its meridianal splendour begins from that instant its downward course.

The reaction was not long in manifesting itself. Usually in such matters there is a pause before the great driving-wheels reverse their motion, and the backward motion, beginning slowly, gathers way as it progresses. But in this case human intelligence and not soulless machinery was the propulsive force of reaction. The speculators had begun to work before the onward movement had come to an end or even begun to slacken. They were loaded up with a vast amount of stocks whose value, even if there had been money to redeem them, was severely limited, whereas they had purchased at prices varying between the first rise above nominal value and that reached by the last desperate speculator. It is not wise to hold such inflated stock too long, and in a crisis sailing-master Wisdom orders Quarter-master Caution to take a trick at the helm. When the bare idea of unification of financial interests was mooted, the wise holders of stock commenced to unload. When this movement began its progress was rapid—so long as there was anything to be moved. The first class to feel it were the bankers. The specie ran out like the pent-up water from a burst reservoir, till in an incredibly short time there was not sufficient remaining to afford the money-change needed in daily life. The advisers and officials of the State, seriously alarmed, began at once to take strong measures supported by royal decrees. Then as ruin began to stare the whole nation in the face more and more with every hour, desperate expedients were resorted to. The value of the currency was made by every stratagem, dishonest trick, and unscrupulous exercise of power, to fluctuate so that such differences or margins as arose might be grasped forthwith for national use. Payments in bullion, except for very small amounts, were forbidden. The possession of anything over five hundred livres in specie was deemed an offence punishable by confiscation, partial or wholesale, and by fine. Domiciliary visits were paid to seek evidence of offence and to enforce the new laws, and informers in this connection were well paid.

Then began a war, between public oppression and individual trickery, to defend acquired rights and evade unjust demands.

The holders of paper money, unable to realise in specie, tried to protect themselves by purchasing goods of intrinsic value. Precious metals, jewels, and such like were bought in such quantities that the supplies diminished and the prices grew, until to avoid immediate ruin, such purchases were proclaimed illegal and prohibited. Then ordinary commodities of lesser values were tried as means of barter, till their prices too rose to such an extent that trade was paralysed. In order to meet the growing danger a still more desperate expedient was resorted to. A decree was issued the effect of which would be to reduce—gradually it was hoped—the obligation of bank notes to one-half their nominal value. This completed the panic, for here was a position which could not be guarded against by any prudence or wisdom. No one could henceforth by any possibility be financially safe. The speculators who had already realised were alone safe. Bona fide investors, if not already overwhelmed by disaster, saw the tide of ruin rising rapidly around them. Nothing within the power of the state could now be done to check or even lessen the state of panic; not even the reversal of the late decree in ten days after its issue. To make matters still worse the Banque at this very time suspended payment. Probably in a wild endeavour to do something which would avert odium from itself by saddling the responsibility on someone else, the Government procured the dismissal of Law from the Controller-Generalship of Finance. However—strange to say—he was very soon appointed by the Regent as Intendant-General of Commerce and Director of the ruined bank. The much-vaunted, idolised, and believed-in "System" had now fallen hopelessly and was ruined forever. Law was everywhere attacked and insulted with such unmitigated rancour that he had to leave the country. He had invested the bulk of the great fortune which he had by now acquired, in estates in France; and these together with everything else that he had were now confiscated.

At the end of the same year, 1720, whilst he was at Brussels he was asked by the command of the Czar (Peter), to administer the finances of Russia, but declined. After this episode, grateful to a broken man, he spent a couple of years wandering about Italy and Germany and probably gaining a fluctuating income through gambling. Next he was to be found in Copenhagen where he had sought sanctuary from his creditors. Next year there was an outward change in his status, when he went to England, on a ship of war, at the invitation of the Government. There he was presented to George I. Somewhat to his chagrin he was denounced in the House of Lords as a Catholic—(he had abjured his old belief of Protestantism before accepting the high office of Controller-General of Finances in 1720)—and an adherent of the Pretender. He pleaded in the King's Bench the Royal pardon for the murder of Beau Austin which had been sent to him in 1719. He spent the succeeding few years in England whence he corresponded with the Duke of Orleans. He expected to be recalled to France but his hope was never realised. He wished to go to the Continent but was practically a prisoner in England, fearing to leave it lest he should be arrested by his creditors, amongst whom was the new French East India Company which had been reconstructed on the ruins of the old. In 1725 Sir Robert Walpole, then Prime Minister, asked Lord Townshend, the Secretary of State, to give Law a King's commission of some sort, so that such might serve for his protection. In the same year he went to Italy. He died in Venice in 1729, in what, compared with his former state, was poverty. To the last he was a gambler, always ready to take long risks for a prospect, however remote, of large gain. A story is told that in his last years he wagered his last thousand pounds to a shilling (20,000 to 1) against the throwing of double sixes six consecutive times. The law of chances was with him and naturally he won. He renewed his wager but the authorities would not allow the further gamble to take place.

John Law married, quite early in life, the daughter of the Earl of Banbury and widow of Mr. Seignior. His widow died in 1747. Some of the members of his family were not undistinguished; his son died a Colonel in the Austrian service; and one of his nephews became Comte de Lauriston and rose to be a General in the French army and Aide-de-Camp to the first Napoleon. He was made a Marshal of France by Louis XVIII.

John Law was a handsome and distinguished-looking man, blonde, with small dark grey eyes and fresh complexion. He made an agreeable impression on strangers. Saint-Simon, the social historian, gave him a good character: "innocent of greed and knavery, a mild good man whom fortune had not spoilt." Others of his time regarded him as a pioneer of modern statesmanship.

How is it then that such a man must be set down an impostor? In historical perspective as an impostor he must be regarded, though not as such in the narrowest view. The answer is that his very prominence sits amongst his judges. Lesser men, and greater men of lesser position, might well stand excused in matters wherein he is accorded condemnation.

"That in the Captain's but a choleric word

Which in the soldier is flat blasphemy."

If, when a man plays a game wherein life and death and the fortunes of many thousands are involved, it behoves him to be at least careful, much greater is his responsibility where the prosperity and happiness of nations are at stake. Had Law merely started new theories of finance, and had they gone wrong, he might well claim, and be ac- corded, excuse. But his were inventions of what, in modern slang, is called "get-rich-quick" principles. Not only did Law not enrich human life—with one exception, that of enlarging the currency in use—or add to the sum total of human well-being and happiness; he even neglected to show that forethought and consideration for others which in all honour ought to be exercised by the deviser and controller of great risks. He was a gambler, and a gambler only. He merely put into the pockets of some persons that which he had taken out of the pockets of others; and in doing so showed no consideration for the poor, the thrifty, the needy—for any of those whose contentment and happiness depend on such as are in high places and dowered in some way with productive powers. The soulless uneducated churl who does an honest day's work does more for humanity than the genius who merely shifts about the already garnered wealth of ages. John Law posed as a benefactor and accepted all the benefits that accrued to him from the praises of those who followed in his wake and gleaned the rich wastage of his empire-moving theories and schemes. Financiers of Law's type no more benefit a country or enrich a people than do the hordes of wasters and "tape"-betting men who prey on labour as locusts do on the crops. If they wish not to do unnecessary harm—which is putting their duty at the lowest possible estimate—they should at least try to avoid repeating the errors which have wrecked others. A brief glance at the wreckage which lay well within the Scotch gambler's vision, will show how he shut his eyes deliberately not only to facts, but to the many correlations of cause and effect. Before his Mississippi Scheme was formulated, there had been experience of banking enterprises, of schemes for mercantile combination and for the exploitation of capital, of adventurous dealings in the developments of countries new and more or less savage, East and West and South.

The following list will typify. Of all these John Law had knowledge sufficient to judge of difficulties to be encountered in the early stages, of dangers not only incidental to the things themselves, but based deep in human nature.

The East India Company founded in 1600

The Bank of England founded in 1694

The Africa Company founded in 1695

The Darien Company founded in 1695

A glance at each of these, all of which were within the scope and knowledge of Law, their aims, formation and development, up to the time spoken of, can hardly fail to be illuminative. The sixteenth century had been an age of adventure and discovery; the seventeenth of the foundation of great commercial enterprise, of conception of ideas, of the constructive beginnings of things. The time for development had come with the eighteenth; and now care and forethought, prudence and resource, were the preparations for success.

The East India Company was in reality the pioneer of corporate trading, and as for nearly a hundred years it was in a measure alone in its scale of magnitude, its experiences could well serve as exemplar, guide, and danger signal. It was based on that surest of all undertakings, natural growth. It came into existence because it was wanted, and from no other cause. Its very name, its modest capital, its self-protective purpose make for understanding.

In its Charter of Incorporation its purpose was indicated in the name: "The Governor and Company of Merchants of London trading to the East Indies." Its capital was £70,000, which though a large sum for those days, was, according to our modern lights, an almost ridiculously small sum for the object then before it, and to which it ultimately attained. The time was ripe for just such an undertaking.

The Peace of Vervins (1598) which left both France and Spain free to look after their domestic concerns, was immediately followed by the Edict of Nantes (1599) which gave religious liberty to France, and such a new freedom is always followed by national expansion. By this time Spain—the explorer or conqueror—and Holland—the patient organiser—held Eastern commerce in their hands. England had been gradually making a commerce of her own in the Indies, and all that was required was an official acknowledgment, so that the thunder of her guns should, when required, follow the creaking of her cordage. From the story of this great enterprise, through its first twenty-five years, could be drawn the lesson of such schemes as Law was now formulating. Though it had succeeded, in spite of Dutch and Portuguese opposition, in establishing "factories" when the historic massacre by the Dutch at Amboyna in the Molucca Islands, took place in 1725, the Eastern Company seemed near its dissolution. It was not till the establishment of the Hooghly factory in 1742 that things began to look up. After that, fortune favoured the Company more than she had appeared likely to do at the start. The marriage of Charles II to Catherine of Braganza in 1661 brought progress in its train. Catherine's dower, which included Bombay and so put a part of Portugal's later possessions in British keeping, greatly stimulated the East India Company which thenceforth was able to weather the storms that threatened or assailed. The privilege of making war on its own account, conceded by Charles II, gave the Company a national importance which was destined to consolidate its interests with those of England itself. So strong did it become that before the end of the eighteenth century it was able to resist the attack on its charter made by a powerful and progressive rival, the "New Company." The rivals, after a few years of pourparlers and tentative efforts, were united in 1708; and thenceforth the amalgamation, under the title "The United Company of Merchants of England trading to the East Indies," was practically unassailable on its own account. It was additionally safe in that it had the protection of the great

Whig Party under Godolphin. The capital of the Company, now enlarged to £3,200,000, was lent to the Government at five per cent, interest and was finally merged in the National Funds. The history of the Company, after 1717 does not belong here, as it is only considered as showing that John Law had the experience of an earlier Company similar to his own to guide him in its management if he had chosen to avail himself of it.

The Bank of England was, strangely enough, the project of a Scotchman, William Paterson. The plan was submitted to Government in 1691 but was not carried into existence for three years. It was purely a business concern, brought into effective existence through the needs of commerce, the opportunity afforded being the need of the State and the concern of the statesman. It had a capital at first of over £1,200,000, which was loaned to the nation on the security of the taxes when the Charter was signed, there being certain safeguards against the possibility of political misuse. The Controlling Board was to have twenty-five members who were to be elected annually by the stockholders with a substantial qualification. There were at this time in England private banks; but this was an effort to formulate the banking rights, duties, and powers of capital under the aegis of the State itself. But even so sound a venture, enormously popular from the very first and with the whole might of the nation behind it, had its own difficulties to encounter. Its instantaneous success was an incentive to other adventurers; and the co-operation with government which it made manifest created jealousy with private persons and commercial concerns. Within two years its very existence was threatened, first by the individual hostility of those in the bullion trade, who already acted as bankers, and then by a rival concern incorporated under strong political support. This was the National Land Bank whose purpose was to use the security of real estate as a guarantee for the paper money which it issued for convenient usage. Strong as the Bank of England was by its nature, its popularity, and its support, it was in actual danger until the rival which had never "caught on"—to use an apposite Americanism—actually and almost instantaneously collapsed.

The safety thus temporarily obtained was purchased at the cost to the Government of a further loan of two million sterling—with the value to the contra of an alliance thus begun with the Whig ministry.

A further danger came from the mad and maddening South Sea Scheme five years later; but from which it was happily saved solely through the greater cupidity and daring of the newer company.

The Darien Company, which followed hard on the heels of The African Company, was formed in 1695, by Paterson; on the base of An Act of the Scottish Parliament for the purpose of making an opening for Scottish capital after the manner of the East India Company by which English enterprise had already so largely benefited. Its career was of such short duration and its failure so complete that there was little difficulty in understanding the causes of its collapse. It might serve for a pendant of Lamb's criticism of the meat that was "ill fed and ill killed, ill kept and ill cooked." The Company was started to utilise, in addition to exploiting new lands, the waste of time, energy and capital, between West and East; and yet it was not till the first trading fleet was sailing that its objective was made known to the adventurers. Its ideas of trading were those of a burlesque, and its materials of barter with tropical savages on the criminal side of the ludicrous—bibles, heavy woollen stuffs and periwigs! Naturally a couple of years finished its working existence and "The rest is silence." And yet at the inception of the scheme two great nations vied with one another for its control.

There are those who may say that John Law was not an

impostor, but a great financier who made a mistake. Financiers must not make mistakes—or else they must be classed amongst the impostors; for they deal with the goods and prospects of others as well as their own. Law was simply a gambler on a great scale. He led a nation, through its units, to believe that the following of his ideas would lead to success. Financial schemes without good ideas and practical working to carry them out are deceptive and destructive. The Mississippi Scheme is a case in point. If the original intention had been carried out in its entirety—which involved vast pioneering and executive action of present and future generations, and an almost absolute foregoing of immediate benefits—the result would have been of immense service to the successors in title of the original ventures. The assessable value of the real estate conveyed under the Mississippi Scheme today equals more than a third of the present gigantic National Debt of France, swollen though the latter is by the Napoleonic wars, the war with Austria, the cost and indemnity of the war with Germany, and, in addition, by the long wars with England and Russia.

If human beings had been angels, content with the prospect of gains in the distant future, Law's schemes might have succeeded. As it was, he, working for his own purposes with an imperfect humanity, can only be judged by results.

WASHINGTON IRVING

THE GREAT MISSISSIPPI BUBBLE

from

Chronicles of Wolfert's Roost and Other Papers

(1855)

WASHINGTON IRVING

THE GREAT MISSISSIPPI BUBBLE

THE GREAT MISSISSIPPI BUBBLE

In the course of a voyage from England, I once fell in with a convoy of merchant ships bound for the West Indies. The weather was uncommonly bland; and the ships vied with each other in spreading sail to catch a light, favoring breeze, until their hulls were almost hidden beneath a cloud of canvas. The breeze went down with the sun, and his last yellow rays shone upon a thousand sails, idly flapping against the masts.

I exulted in the beauty of the scene, and augured a prosperous voyage; but the veteran master of the ship shook his head, and pronounced this halcyon calm a "weather-breeder." And so it proved. A storm burst forth in the night; the sea roared and raged; and when the day broke, I beheld the late gallant convoy scattered in every direction; some dismasted, others scudding under bare poles, and many firing signals of distress.

I have since been occasionally reminded of this scene, by those calm, sunny seasons in the commercial world, which are known by the name of "times of unexampled prosperity." They are the sure weather-breeders of traffic. Every now and then the world is visited by one of these delusive seasons, when "the credit system," as it is called, expands to full luxuriance, everybody trusts everybody; a bad debt is a thing unheard of; the broad way to certain and sudden wealth lies plain and open;

and men are tempted to dash forward boldly, from the facility of borrowing.

Promissory notes, interchanged between scheming individuals, are liberally discounted at the banks, which become so many mints to coin words into cash; and as the supply of words is inexhaustible, it may readily be supposed what a vast amount of promissory capital is soon in circulation. Every one now talks in thousands; nothing is heard but gigantic operations in trade; great purchases and sales of real property, and immense sums made at every transfer. All, to be sure, as yet exists in promise; but the believer in promises calculates the aggregate as solid capital, and falls back in amazement at the amount of public wealth, the "unexampled state of public prosperity."

Now is the time for speculative and dreaming or designing men. They relate their dreams and projects to the ignorant and credulous, dazzle them with golden visions, and set them madding after shadows. The example of one stimulates another; speculation rises on speculation; bubble rises on bubble; every one helps with his breath to swell the windy superstructure, and admires and wonders at the magnitude of the inflation he has contributed to produce.

Speculation is the romance of trade, and casts contempt upon all its sober realities. It renders the stock-jobber a magician, and the exchange a region of enchantment. It elevates the merchant into a kind of knight errant, or rather a commercial Quixote. The slow but sure gains of snug percentage become despicable in his eyes; no "operation" is thought worthy of attention that does not double or treble the investment. No business is worth following that does not promise an immediate fortune. As he sits musing over his ledger, with pen behind his ear, he is like La Mancha's hero in his study, dreaming over his books of chivalry. His dusty counting-house fades before his eyes, or changes into a Spanish mine; he gropes after diamonds, or dives after pearls. The subterranean garden of Aladdin is nothing to the realms of wealth that break upon his imagination.

Could this delusion always last, the life of a merchant would indeed be a golden dream; but it is as short as it is brilliant. Let but a doubt enter, and the "season of unexampled prosperity" is at end. The coinage of words is suddenly curtailed; the promissory capital begins to vanish into smoke; a panic succeeds, and the whole superstructure, built upon credit and reared by speculation, crumbles to the ground, leaving scarce a wreck behind:

"It is such stuff as dreams are made of."

When a man of business, therefore, hears on every side rumors of fortunes suddenly acquired; when he finds banks liberal, and brokers busy; when he sees adventurers flush of paper capital, and full of scheme and enterprise; when he perceives a greater disposition to buy than to sell; when trade overflows its accustomed channels and deluges the country; when he hears of new regions of commercial adventure; of distant marts and distant mines, swallowing merchandise and disgorging gold; when he finds joint-stock companies of all kinds forming; railroads, canals, and locomotive engines, springing up on every side; when idlers suddenly become men of business, and dash into the game of commerce as they would into the hazards of the faro table; when he beholds the streets glittering with new equipages, palaces conjured up by the magic of speculation; tradesmen flushed with sudden success, and vying with each other in ostentatious expense; in a word, when he hears the whole community joining in the theme of "unexampled prosperity," let him look upon the whole as a "weather-breeder," and prepare for the impending storm.

The foregoing remarks are intended merely as a prelude to a narrative I am about to lay before the public, of one of the most memorable instances of the infatuation of gain to be found in the whole history of commerce. I allude to the famous Mississippi Bubble. It is a matter that has passed into a proverb, and become a phrase in every one's mouth, yet of which not one merchant in ten has probably a distinct idea. I have therefore thought that an authentic account of it would be interesting and salutary, at the present moment, when we are suffering under the effects of a severe access of the credit system, and just recovering from one of its ruinous delusions.

Before entering into the story of this famous chimera, it is proper to give a few particulars concerning the individual who engendered it. John Law was born in Edinburgh in 1671. His father, William Law, was a rich goldsmith, and left his son an estate of considerable value, called Lauriston, situated about four miles from Edinburgh. Goldsmiths, in those days, acted occasionally as bankers, and his father's operations, under this character, may have originally turned the thoughts of the youth to the science of calculation, in which he became an adept; so that at an early age he excelled in playing at all games of combination.

In 1694 he appeared in London, where a handsome person, and an easy and insinuating address, gained him currency in the first circles and the nickname of "Beau Law." The same personal advantages gave him success in the world of gallantry, until he became involved in a quarrel with Beau Wilson, his rival in fashion, whom he killed in a duel, and then fled to France, to avoid prosecution.

He returned to Edinburgh in 1700, and remained there several years; during which time he first broached his great credit system, offering to supply the deficiency of coin by the establishment of a bank, which, according to his views, might emit a paper currency equivalent to the whole landed estate of the kingdom.

His scheme excited great astonishment in Edinburgh; but, though the government was not sufficiently advanced in financial knowledge to detect the fallacies upon which it was founded, Scottish caution and suspicion served in the place of wisdom, and the project was rejected. Law met with no better success with the English Parliament; and the fatal affair of the death of Wilson still hanging over him, for which he had never been able to procure a pardon, he again went to France.

The financial affairs of France were at this time in a deplorable condition. The wars, the pomp and profusion, of Louis XIV., and his religious persecutions of whole classes of the most industrious of his subjects, had exhausted his treasury, and overwhelmed the nation with debt. The old monarch clung to his selfish magnificence, and could not be induced to diminish his enormous expenditure; and his minister of finance was driven to his wits' end to devise all kinds of disastrous expedients to keep up the royal state, and to extricate the nation from its embarrassments.

In this state of things, Law ventured to bring forward his financial project. It was founded on the plan of the Bank of England, which had already been in successful operation several years. He met with immediate patronage, and a congenial spirit, in the Duke of Orleans, who had married a natural daughter of the King. The Duke had been astonished at the facility with which England had supported the burden of a public debt, created by the wars of Anne and William, and which exceeded in amount that under which France was groaning. The whole matter was soon explained by Law to his satisfaction. The latter maintained that England had stopped at the mere threshold of an art capable of creating unlimited sources of national wealth. The Duke was dazzled with his splendid views and specious reasonings, and thought he clearly comprehended his system. Demarets, the Comptroller-General of Finance, was not so easily deceived. He pronounced the plan of Law more pernicious than any of the disastrous expedients that the government had yet been driven to. The old King also, Louis XIV., detested all innovations, especially those which came from a rival nation; the project of a bank, therefore, was utterly rejected.

Law remained for a while in Paris, leading a gay and affluent existence, owing to his handsome person, easy manners, flexible temper, and a faro-bank which he had set up. His agreeable career was interrupted by a message from D'Argenson, Lieutenant-General of Police, ordering him to quit Paris, alleging that he was "rather too skillful at the game which he had introduced."

For several succeeding years he shifted his residence from state to state of Italy and Germany; offering his scheme of finance to every court that he visited, but without success. The Duke of Savoy, Victor Amadeus, afterward king of Sardinia, was much struck with his project; but after considering it for a time, replied, "I am not sufficiently powerful to ruin myself."

The shifting, adventurous life of Law, and the equivocal means by which he appeared to live, playing high, and always with great success, threw a cloud of suspicion over him wherever he went, and caused him to be expelled by the magistracy from the semi-commercial, semi-aristocratical cities of Venice and Genoa.

The events of 1715 brought Law back again to Paris. Louis XIV. was dead. Louis XV. was a mere child, and during his minority the Duke of Orleans held the reins of government as Regent. Law had at length found his man.

The Duke of Orleans has been differently represented by different contemporaries. He appears to have had excellent natural qualities, perverted by a bad education. He was of the middle size, easy and graceful, with an agreeable countenance, and open, affable demeanor. His mind was quick and sagacious, rather than profound; and his quickness of intellect, and excellence of memory, supplied the lack of studious application. His wit was prompt and pungent; he expressed himself with vivacity and precision; his imagination was vivid, his temperament sanguine and joyous; his courage daring. His mother, the Duchess of Orleans, expressed his character in a jeu d'esprit. "The fairies," said she, "were invited to be present at his birth, and each one conferring a talent on my son, he possesses them all. Unfortunately, we had forgotten to invite an old fairy, who, arriving after all the others, exclaimed, 'He shall have all the talents, excepting that to make a good use of them.'"

Under proper tuition, the Duke might have risen to real greatness; but in his early years he was put under the tutelage of the Abbé Dubois, one of the subtlest and basest spirits that ever intrigued its way into eminent place and power. The Abbé was of low origin and despicable exterior, totally destitute of morals, and perfidious in the extreme; but with a supple, insinuating address, and an accommodating spirit, tolerant of all kinds of profligacy in others. Conscious of his own inherent baseness, he sought to secure an influence over his pupil, by corrupting his principles and fostering his vices; he debased him, to keep himself from being despised. Unfortunately he succeeded. To the early precepts of this infamous pander have been attributed those excesses that disgraced the manhood of the Regent, and gave a licentious character to his whole course of government. His love of pleasure, quickened and indulged by those who should have restrained it, led him into all kinds of sensual indulgence. He had been taught to think lightly of the most serious duties and sacred ties; to turn virtue into a jest, and consider religion mere hypocrisy. He was a gay misanthrope, that had a sovereign but sportive contempt for mankind;

believed that his most devoted servant would be his enemy, if interest prompted; and maintained that an honest man was he who had the art to conceal that he was the contrary.

He surrounded himself with a set of dissolute men like himself; who, let loose from the restraint under which they had been held, during the latter hypocritical days of Louis XIV., now gave way to every kind of debauchery. With these men the Regent used to shut himself up, after the hours of business, and excluding all graver persons and graver concerns, celebrate the most drunken and disgusting orgies; where obscenity and blasphemy formed the seasoning of conversation. For the profligate companions of these revels, he invented the appellation of his roués, the literal meaning of which is men broken on the wheel; intended, no doubt, to express their broken-down characters and dislocated fortunes; although a contemporary asserts that it designated the punishment that most of them merited. Madame de Labran, who was present at one of the Regent's suppers, was disgusted by the conduct and conversation of the host and his guests, and observed, at table, that God, after he had created man, took the refuse clay that was left, and made of it the souls of lackeys and princes.

Such was the man that now ruled the destinies of France. Law found him full of perplexities, from the disastrous state of the finances. He had already tampered with the coinage, calling in the coin of the nation, restamping it, and issuing it at a nominal increase of one-fifth; thus defrauding the nation out of twenty per cent of its capital. He was not likely, therefore, to be scrupulous about any means likely to relieve him from financial difficulties; he had even been led to listen to the cruel alternative of a national bankruptcy.

Under these circumstances, Law confidently brought forward his scheme of a bank, that was to pay off the national debt, increase the revenue, and at the same time diminish the taxes. The following is stated as the theory by which he recommended his system to the Regent. The credit enjoyed by a banker or a merchant, he observed, increases his capital tenfold; that is to say, he who has a capital of one thousand livres, may, if he possess sufficient credit, extend his operations to a million, and reap profits to that amount. In like manner, a state that can collect into a bank all the current coin of the kingdom, would be as powerful as if its capital were increased tenfold. The specie must be drawn into the bank, not by way of loan, or by taxations, but in the way of deposit. This might be effected in different modes, either by inspiring confidence or by exerting authority. One mode, he observed, had already been in use. Each time that a state makes a recoinage, it becomes momentarily the depositary of all the money called in, belonging to the subjects of that state. His bank was to effect the same purpose; that is to say, to receive in deposit all the coin of the kingdom, but to give in exchange its bills, which, being of an invariable value, bearing an interest, and being payable on demand, would not only supply the place of coin, but prove a better and more profitable currency.

The Regent caught with avidity at the scheme. It suited his bold, reckless spirit, and his grasping extravagance. Not that he was altogether the dupe of Law's specious projects; still he was apt, like many other men, unskilled in the arcana of finance, to mistake the multiplication of money for the multiplication of wealth; not understanding that it was a mere agent or instrument in the interchange of traffic, to represent the value of the various productions of industry; and that an increased circulation of coin or bank bills, in the shape of currency, only adds a proportionably increased and fictitious value to such productions. Law enlisted the vanity of the Regent in his cause. He persuaded him that he saw more clearly than others into sublime theories of finance, which were quite above the ordinary apprehension. He used to declare that, excepting the Regent and the Duke of Savoy, no one had thoroughly comprehended his system.

It is certain that it met with strong opposition from the Regent's ministers, the Duke de Noailles and the Chancellor d'Anguesseau; and it was no less strenuously opposed by the Parliament of Paris. Law, however, had a potent though secret coadjutor in the Abbé Dubois, now rising, during the regency, into great political power, and who retained a baneful influence over the mind of the Regent. This wily priest, as avaricious as he was ambitious, drew large sums from Law as subsidies, and aided him greatly in many of his most pernicious operations. He aided him, in the present instance, to fortify the mind of the Regent against all the remonstrances of his ministers and the parliament.

Accordingly, on the 2d of May, 1716, letters patent were granted to Law, to establish a bank of deposit, discount, and circulation, under the firm of "Law and Company," to continue for twenty years. The capital was fixed at six millions of livres, divided into shares of five hundred livres each, which were to be sold for twenty-five per cent of the Regent's debased coin, and seventy-five per cent of the public securities; which were then at a great reduction from their nominal value, and which then amounted to nineteen hundred millions. The ostensible object of the bank, as set forth in the patent, was to encourage the commerce and manufactures of France. The louis d'ors and crowns of the bank were always to retain the same standard of value, and its bills to be payable in them on demand.

At the outset, while the bank was limited in its operations, and while its paper really represented the specie in its vaults, it seemed to realize all that had been promised from it. It rapidly acquired public confidence, and an extended circulation, and produced an activity in commerce unknown under the baneful government of Louis XIV. As the bills of the bank bore an interest, and as it was stipulated they would be of invariable value, and as hints had been artfully circulated that the coin would experience successive diminution, everybody hastened to the bank to exchange gold and silver for paper. So great became the throng of depositors, and so intense their eagerness, that there was quite a press and struggle at the bank door, and a ludicrous panic was awakened, as if there was danger of their not being admitted. An anecdote of the time relates that one of the clerks, with an ominous smile, called out to the struggling multitude, "Have a little patience, my friends; we mean to take all your money;" an assertion disastrously verified in the sequel.

Thus, by the simple establishment of a bank, Law and the Regent obtained pledges of confidence for the consummation of further and more complicated schemes, as yet hidden from the public. In a little while, the bank shares rose enormously, and the amount of its notes in circulation exceeded one hundred and ten millions of livres. A subtle stroke of policy had rendered it popular with the aristocracy. Louis XIV. had several years previously imposed an income tax of a tenth, giving his royal word that it should cease in 1717. This tax had been exceedingly irksome to the privileged orders; and in the present disastrous times they had dreaded an augmentation of it. In consequence of the successful operation of Law's scheme, however, the tax was abolished, and now nothing was to be heard among the nobility and clergy but praises of the Regent and the bank.

Hitherto all had gone well, and all might have continued to go well, had not the paper system been further expanded. But Law had yet the grandest part of his scheme to develop. He had to open his ideal world of speculation, his El Dorado of unbounded wealth. The English had brought the vast imaginary commerce of the South Seas in aid of their banking operations. Law sought to bring, as an immense auxiliary of his bank, the whole trade of the Mississippi. Under this name was included not merely the river so called, but the vast region known as Louisiana, extending from north latitude 29° up to Canada in north latitude 40°. This country had been granted by Louis XIV. to the Sieur Crozat, but he had been induced to resign his patent. In conformity to the plea of Mr. Law, letters patent were granted in August, 1717, for the creation of a commercial company, which was to have the colonizing of this country, and the monopoly of its trade and resources, and of the beaver or fur trade with Canada. It was called the Western, but became better known as the Mississippi Company. The capital was fixed at one hundred millions of livres, divided into shares, bearing an Interest of four per cent, which were subscribed for in the public securities. As the bank was to co-operate with the company, the Regent ordered that its bills should be received the same as coin, in all payments of the public revenue. Law was appointed chief director of this company, which was an exact copy of the Earl of Oxford's South Sea Company, set on foot in 1711, and which distracted all England with the frenzy of speculation. In like manner with the delusive picturings given in that memorable scheme of the sources of rich trade to be opened in the South Sea countries, Law held forth magnificent prospects of the fortunes to be made in colonizing Louisiana, which was represented as a veritable land of promise, capable of yielding every variety of the most precious produce. Reports, too, were artfully circulated, with great mystery, as if to the "chosen few," of mines of gold and silver recently discovered in Louisiana, and which would insure instant wealth to the early purchasers. These confidential whispers of course soon became public; and were confirmed by travelers fresh from the Mississippi, and doubtless bribed, who had seen the mines in question, and declared them superior in richness to those of Mexico and Peru. Nay, more, ocular proof was furnished to public credulity, in ingots of gold conveyed to the mint, as if just brought from the mines of Louisiana.

Extraordinary measures were adopted to force a colonization. An edict was issued to collect and transport settlers to the Mississippi. The police lent its aid. The streets and prisons of Paris, and of the provincial cities, were swept of mendicants and vagabonds of all kinds, who were conveyed to Havre de Grace. About six thousand were crowded into ships, where no precautions had been taken for their health or accommodation. Instruments of all kinds proper for the working of mines were ostentatiously paraded in public, and put on board the vessels; and the whole set sail for this fabled El Dorado, which was to prove the grave of the greater part of its wretched colonists.

D'Anguesseau, the chancellor, a man of probity and integrity, still lifted his voice against the paper system of Law, and his project of colonization, and was eloquent and prophetic in picturing the evils they were calculated to produce; the private distress and public degradation; the corruption of morals and manners; the triumph of knaves and schemers; the ruin of fortunes, and downfall of families. He was incited more and more to this opposition by the Duke de Noailles, the Minister of Finance, who was jealous of the growing ascendency of Law over the mind of the Regent, but was less honest than the chancellor in his opposition. The Regent was excessively annoyed by the difficulties they conjured up in the way of his darling schemes of finance, and the countenance they gave to the opposition of parliament; which body, disgusted more and more with the abuses of the regency, and the system of Law, had gone so far as to carry its remonstrances to the very foot of the throne.

He determined to relieve himself from these two ministers, who, either through honesty or policy, interfered with all his plans. Accordingly, on the 28th of January, 1718, he dismissed the chancellor from office, and exiled him to his estate in the country; and shortly afterward removed the Duke de Noailles from the administration of the finances.

The opposition of parliament to the Regent and his measures was carried on with increasing violence. That body aspired to an equal authority with the Regent in the administration of affairs, and pretended, by its decree, to suspend an edict of the regency, ordering a new coinage and altering the value of the currency. But its chief hostility was leveled against Law, a foreigner and a heretic, and one who was considered by a majority of the members in the light of a malefactor. In fact, so far was this hostility carried, that secret measures were taken to investigate his malversations, and to collect evidence against him; and it was resolved in parliament that, should the testimony collected justify their suspicions, they would have him seized and brought before them; would give him a brief trial, and, if convicted, would hang him in the courtyard of the palace, and throw open the gates after the execution, that the public might behold his corpse!

Law received intimation of the danger hanging over him, and was in terrible trepidation. He took refuge in the Palais Royal, the residence of the Regent, and implored his protection. The Regent himself was embarrassed by the sturdy opposition of parliament, which contemplated nothing less than a decree reversing most of his public measures, especially those of finance. His indecision kept Law for a time in an agony of terror and suspense. Finally, by assembling a board of justice, and bringing to his aid the absolute authority of the King, he triumphed over parliament and relieved Law from his dread of being hanged.

The system now went on with flowing sail. The Western or Mississippi Company, being identified with the bank, rapidly increased in power and privileges. One monopoly after another was granted to it; the trade of the Indian seas; the slave trade with Senegal and Guinea; the farming of tobacco; the national coinage, etc. Each new privilege was made a pretext for issuing more bills, and caused an immense advance in the price of stock. At length, on the 4th of December, 1718, the Regent gave the establishment the imposing title of 'The Royal Bank,' and proclaimed that he had effected the purchase of all the shares, the proceeds of which he had added to its capital This measure seemed to shock the public feeling more than any other connected with the system, and roused the indignation of parliament. The French nation had been so accustomed to attach an idea of everything noble, lofty, and magnificent to the royal name and person, especially during the stately and sumptuous reign of Louis XIV., that they could not at first tolerate the idea of royalty being in any degree mingled with matters of traffic and finance, and the King being in a manner a banker. It was one of the downward steps, however, by which royalty lost its illusive splendor in France, and became gradually cheapened in the public mind.

Arbitrary measures now began to be taken to force the bills of the bank into artificial currency. On the 27th of December appeared an order in council, forbidding, under severe penalties, the payment of any sum above six hundred livres in gold or silver. This decree rendered bank bills necessary in all transactions of purchase and sale, and called for a new emission. The prohibition was occasionally evaded or opposed; confiscations were the consequence; informers were rewarded, and spies and traitors began to spring up in all the domestic walks of life.

The worst effect of this illusive system was the mania for gain, or rather for gambling in stocks, that now seized upon the whole nation. Under the exciting effects of lying reports, and the forcing effects of government decrees, the shares of the company went on rising in value until they reached thirteen hundred per cent. Nothing was now spoken of but the price of shares, and the immense fortunes suddenly made by lucky speculators. Those whom Law had deluded used every means to delude others. The most extravagant dreams were indulged, concerning the wealth to flow in upon the company from its colonies, its trade, and its various monopolies. It is true nothing as yet had been realized, nor could in some time be realized, from these distant sources, even if productive; but the imaginations of speculators are ever in the advance, and their conjectures are immediately converted into facts. Lying reports now flew from mouth to month, of sure avenues to fortune suddenly thrown open. The more extravagant the fable, the more readily was it believed. To doubt was to awaken anger, or incur ridicule. In a time of public infatuation, it requires no small exercise of courage to doubt a popular fallacy.

Paris now became the center of attraction for the adventurous and the avaricious, who flocked to it, not merely from the provinces, but from neighboring countries. A stock exchange was established in a house in the Rue Quincampoix, and became immediately the gathering place of stock-jobbers. The exchange opened at seven o'clock, with the beat of drum and sound of bell, and closed at night with the same signals. Guards were stationed at each end of the street, to maintain order and exclude carriages and horses. The whole street swarmed throughout the day like a bee-hive. Bargains of all kinds were seized upon with avidity. Shares of stock passed from hand to hand, mounting in value, one knew not why. Fortunes were made in a moment, as if by magic; and every lucky bargain prompted those around to a more desperate throw of the die. The fever went on, increasing in intensity as the day declined; and when the drum beat, and the bell rang, at night, to close the exchange, there were exclamations of impatience and despair, as if the wheel of fortune had suddenly been stopped when about to make its luckiest evolution.

To engulf all classes in this ruinous vortex, Law now split the shares of fifty millions of stock each into one hundred shares; thus, as in the splitting of lottery tickets, accommodating the venture to the humblest purse. Society was thus stirred up to its very dregs, and adventurers of the lowest order hurried to the stock market. All honest, industrious pursuits, and modest gains, were now despised. Wealth was to be obtained instantly, without labor and without stint. The upper classes were as base in their venality as the lower. The highest and most powerful nobles, abandoning all generous pursuits and lofty aims, engaged in the vile scuffle for gam. They were even baser than the lower classes; for some of them, who were members of the council of the regency, abused their station and their influence, and promoted measures by which shares rose while in their hands, and they made immense profits.

The Duke de Bourbon, the Prince of Conti, the Dukes de la Force and D'Antin were among the foremost of these illustrious stock-jobbers. They were nicknamed the Mississippi Lords, and they smiled at the sneering title. In fact, the usual distinctions of society had lost their consequence, under the reign of this new passion. Bank, talent, military fame, no longer inspired deference. All respect for others, all self-respect, were forgotten in the mercenary struggle of the stock-market. Even prelates and ecclesiastical corporations, forgetting their true objects of devotion, mingled among the votaries of Mammon. They were not behind those who wielded the civil power in fabricating ordinances suited to their avaricious purposes. Theological decisions forthwith appeared, in which the anathema launched by the Church against usury was conveniently construed as not extending to the traffic in bank shares!

The Abbé Dubois entered into the mysteries of stockjobbing

with all the zeal of an apostle, and enriched himself by the spoils of the credulous; and he continually drew large sums from Law, as considerations for his political influence. Faithless to his country, in the course of his gambling speculations he transferred to England a great amount of specie, which had been paid into the royal treasury; thus contributing to the subsequent dearth of the precious metals.

The female sex participated in this sordid frenzy. Princesses of the blood, and ladies of the highest nobility, were among the most rapacious of stock-jobbers. The Regent seemed to have the riches of Croesus at his command, and lavished money by hundreds of thousands upon his female relatives and favorites, as well as upon his roués, the dissolute companions of his debauches. "My son," writes the Regent's mother, in her correspondence, "gave me shares to the amount of two millions, which I distributed among my household. The King also took several millions for his own household. All the royal family have had them; all the children and grandchildren of France, and the princes of the blood."

Luxury and extravagance kept pace with this sudden inflation of fancied wealth. The hereditary palaces of nobles were pulled down, and rebuilt on a scale of augmented splendor. Entertainments were given of incredible cost and magnificence. Never before had been such display in houses, furniture, equipages, and amusements. This was particularly the case among persons of the lower ranks, who had suddenly become possessed of millions. Ludicrous anecdotes are related of some of these upstarts. One, who had just launched a splendid carriage, when about to use it for the first time, instead of getting in at the door, mounted, through habitude, to his accustomed place behind. Some ladies of quality, seeing a well-dressed woman covered with diamonds, but whom nobody knew, alight from a very handsome carriage, inquired who she was of the footman.

He replied, with a sneer: "It is a lady who has recently tumbled from a garret into this carriage." Mr. Law's domestics were said to become in like manner suddenly enriched by the crumbs that fell from his table. His coachman, having made his fortune, retired from his service. Mr. Law requested him to procure a coachman in his place. He appeared the next day with two, whom he pronounced equally good, and told Mr. Law: "Take which of them you choose, and I will take the other!"

Nor were these *novi homini* treated with the distance and disdain they would formerly have experienced from the haughty aristocracy of France. The pride of the old noblesse had been stifled by the stronger instinct of avarice. They rather sought the intimacy and confidence of these lucky upstarts; and it has been observed that a nobleman would gladly take his seat at the table of the fortunate lackey of yesterday, in hopes of learning from him the secret of growing rich!

Law now went about with a countenance radiant with success and apparently dispensing wealth on every side. "He is admirably skilled in all that relates to finance," writes the Duchess of Orleans, the Regent's mother, "and has put the affairs of the state in such good order that all the King's debts have been paid. He is so much run after that he has no repose night or day. A duchess even kissed his hand publicly. If a duchess can do this, what will other ladies do?"

Wherever he went, his path, we are told, was beset by a sordid throng, who waited to see him pass, and sought to obtain the favor of a word, a nod, or smile, as if a mere glance from him would bestow fortune. When at home, his house was absolutely besieged by furious candidates for fortune. "They forced the doors," says the Duke de St. Simon; "they scaled his windows from the garden; they made their way into his cabinet down the chimney!"

The same venal court was paid by all classes to his family. The highest ladies of the court vied with each other in meannesses to purchase the lucrative friendship of Mrs. Law and her daughter. They waited upon them with as much assiduity and adulation as if they had been princesses of the blood. The Regent one day expressed a desire that some duchess should accompany his daughter to Genoa. "My lord," said some one present, "if you would have a choice from among the duchesses, you need but send to Mrs. Law's, you will find them all assembled there."

The wealth of Law rapidly increased with the expansion of the bubble. In the course of a few months he purchased fourteen titled estates, paying for them in paper; and the public hailed these sudden and vast acquisitions of landed property as so many proofs of the soundness of his system. In one instance he met with a shrewd bargainer, who had not the general faith in his paper money. The President de Novion insisted on being paid for an estate in hard coin. Law accordingly brought the amount, four hundred thousand livres, in specie, saying, with a sarcastic smile, that he preferred paying in money as its weight rendered it a mere encumbrance. As it happened, the president could give no clear title to the land, and the money had to be refunded. He paid it back in paper, which Law dared not refuse, lest he should depreciate it in the market.

The course of illusory credit went on triumphantly for eighteen months. Law had nearly fulfilled one of his promises, for the greater part of the public debt had been paid off; but how paid? In bank shares, which had been trumped up several hundred per cent above their value, and which were to vanish like smoke in the hands of the holders.

One of the most striking attributes of Law was the imperturbable assurance and self-possession with which he replied to every objection, and found a solution for every problem. He had the dexterity of a juggler in evading difficulties; and what was peculiar, made figures themselves, which are the very elements of exact demonstration, the means to dazzle and bewilder.

Toward the latter end of 1719 the Mississippi scheme had reached its highest point of glory. Half a million of strangers had crowded into Paris in quest of fortune. The hotels and lodging-houses were overflowing; lodgings were procured with excessive difficulty; granaries were turned into bedrooms; provisions had risen enormously in price; splendid houses were multiplying on every side; the streets were crowded with carriages; above a thousand new equipages had been launched.

On the eleventh of December, Law obtained another prohibitory decree, for the purpose of sweeping all the remaining specie in circulation into the bank. By this it was forbidden to make any payment in silver above ten livres, or in gold above three hundred.

The repeated decrees of this nature, the object of which was to depreciate the value of gold, and increase the illusive credit of paper, began to awaken doubts of a system which required such bolstering. Capitalists gradually awoke from their bewilderment. Sound and able financiers consulted together, and agreed to make common cause against this continual expansion of a paper system. The shares of the bank and of the company began to decline in value. Wary men took the alarm, and began to realize, a word now first brought into use, to express the conversion of ideal property into something real.

The Prince of Conti, one of the most prominent and grasping of the Mississippi lords, was the first to give a blow to the credit of the bank. There was a mixture of ingratitude in his conduct that characterized the venal baseness of the times. He had received from time to time enormous sums from Law, as the price of his influence and patronage. His avarice had increased with every acquisition, until Law was compelled to refuse one of his exactions. In revenge the Prince immediately sent such an amount of paper to the bank to be cashed that it required four wagons to bring away the silver, and he had the meanness to loll out of the window of his hotel and jest and exult as it was trundled into his porte-cochère.

This was the signal for other drains of like nature. The English and Dutch merchants, who had purchased a great amount of bank paper at low prices, cashed them at the bank, and carried the money out of the country. Other strangers did the like, thus draining the kingdom of its specie, and leaving paper in its place.

The Regent, perceiving these symptoms of decay in the system, sought to restore it to public confidence by conferring marks of confidence upon its author.

He accordingly resolved to make Law Comptroller General of the Finances of France. There was a material obstacle in his way. Law was a Protestant, and the Regent, unscrupulous as he was himself, did not dare publicly to outrage the severe edicts which Louis XIV., in his bigot days, had fulminated against all heretics. Law soon let him know that there would be no difficulty on that head. He was ready at any moment to abjure his religion in the way of business. For decency's sake, however, it was judged proper he should previously be convinced and converted. A ghostly instructor was soon found, ready to accomplish his conversion in the shortest possible time. This was the Abbé Tencin, a profligate creature of the profligate Dubois, and like him working his way to ecclesiastical promotion and temporal wealth, by the basest means.

Under the instructions of the Abbé Tencin, Law soon mastered the mysteries and dogmas of the Catholic doctrine; and, after a brief course of ghostly training, declared himself thoroughly convinced and converted. To avoid the sneers and jests of the Parisian public the ceremony of abjuration took place at Melun. Law made a pious present of one hundred thousand livres to the Church of St. Roque, and the Abbé Tencin was rewarded for his edifying labors by sundry shares and bank bills; which he shrewdly took care to convert into cash, having as little faith in the system as in the piety of his new convert. A more grave and moral community might have been outraged by this scandalous farce; but the Parisians laughed at it with their usual levity, and contented themselves with making it the subject of a number of songs and epigrams.

Law now being orthodox in his faith, took out letters of naturalization, and having thus surmounted the intervening obstacles, was elevated by the Regent to the post of comptroller-general. So accustomed had the community become to all juggles and transmutations in this hero of finance, that no one seemed shocked or astonished at his sudden elevation. On the contrary, being now considered perfectly established in place and power, he became more than ever the object of venal adoration. Men of rank and dignity thronged his antechamber, waiting patiently their turn for an audience; and titled dames demeaned themselves to take the front seats of the carriages of his wife and daughter, as if they had been riding with princesses of the blood royal. Law's head grew giddy with his elevation, and he began to aspire after aristocratical distinction. There was to be a court ball, at which several of the young noblemen were to dance in a ballet with the youthful King. Law requested that his son might be admitted into the ballet, and the Regent consented. The young scions of nobility, however, were indignant and scouted the "intruding upstart." Their more worldly parents, fearful of displeasing the modern Midas, reprimanded them in vain. The striplings had not yet imbibed the passion for gain, and still held to their high blood. The son of the banker received slights and annoyances on all sides, and the public applauded them for their spirit. A fit of illness came opportunely to relieve the youth from an honor which would have cost him a world of vexations and affronts.

In February, 1720, shortly after Law's installment in office, a decree came out uniting the bank to the India Company, by which last name the whole establishment was now known. The decree stated that as the bank was royal, the King was bound to make good the value of its bills; that he committed to the company the government of the bank for fifty years, and sold to it fifty millions of stock belonging to him, for nine hundred millions; a simple advance of eighteen hundred per cent. The decree further declared, in the King's name, that he would never draw on the bank until the value of his drafts had first been lodged in it by his receivers general.

The bank, it was said, had by this time issued notes to the amount of one thousand millions; being more paper than all the banks of Europe were able to circulate. To aid its credit, the receivers of the revenue were directed to take bank notes of the sub-receivers. All payments, also, of one hundred livres and upward were ordered to be made in banknotes. These compulsory measures for a short time gave a false credit to the bank, which proceeded to discount merchants' notes, to lend money on jewels, plate, and other valuables, as well as on mortgages.

Still further to force on the system an edict next appeared, forbidding any individual, or any corporate body, civil or religious, to hold in possession more than five hundred livres in current coin; that is to say, about seven louis d'ors: the value of the louis-d'or in paper being, at the time, seventy-two livres. All the gold and silver they might have above this pittance was to be brought to the royal bank and exchanged either for shares or bills.

As confiscation was the penalty of disobedience to this decree, and informers were assured a share of the forfeitures, a bounty was in a manner held out to domestic spies and traitors; and the most odious scrutiny was awakened into the pecuniary affairs of families and individuals. The very confidence between friends and relatives was unpaired, and all the domestic ties and virtues of society were threatened, until a general sentiment of indignation broke forth, that compelled the Regent to rescind the odious decree. Lord Stairs, the British ambassador, speaking of the system of espionage encouraged by this edict, observed that it was impossible to doubt that Law was a thorough Catholic, since he had thus established the inquisition, after having already proved transubstantiation, by changing specie into paper.

Equal abuses had taken place under the colonizing project. In his thousand expedients to amass capital, Law had sold parcels of land in Mississippi, at the rate of three thousand livres for a league square. Many capitalists had purchased estates large enough to constitute almost a principality; the only evil was, Law had sold a property which he could not deliver. The agents of police, who aided in recruiting the ranks of the colonists, had been guilty of scandalous impositions. Under pretense of taking up mendicants and vagabonds, they had scoured the streets at night, seizing upon honest mechanics, or their sons, and hurrying them to their crimping-houses, for the sole purpose of extorting money from them as a ransom. The populace was roused to indignation by these abuses. The officers of police were mobbed in the exercise of their odious functions, and several of them were killed; which put an end to this flagrant abuse of power.

In March, a most extraordinary decree of the council fixed the price of shares of the India Company at nine thousand livres each. All ecclesiastical communities and hospitals were now prohibited from investing money at interest, in anything but India stock. With all these props and stays, the system continued to totter. How could it be otherwise, under a despotic government that could alter the value of property at every moment? The very compulsory measures that were adopted to establish the credit of the bank hastened its fall; plainly showing there was a want of solid security.

Law caused pamphlets to be published, setting forth, in eloquent language, the vast profits that must accrue to holders of the stock, and the impossibility of the King's ever doing it any harm. On the very back of these assertions came forth an edict of the King, dated the 22d of May, wherein, under pretense of having reduced the value of his coin, it was declared necessary to reduce the value of his bank-notes one-half, and of the India shares from nine thousand to five thousand livres.

This decree came like a clap of thunder upon shareholders. They found one half of the pretended value of the paper in their hands annihilated in an instant; and what certainty had they with respect to the other half? The rich considered themselves ruined; those in humbler circumstances looked forward to abject beggary.

The parliament seized the occasion to stand forth as the protector of the public, and refused to register the decree. It gained the credit of compelling the Regent to retrace his step, though it is more probable he yielded to the universal burst of public astonishment and reprobation. On the 27th of May the edict was revoked, and bank bills were restored to their previous value. But the fatal blow had been struck; the delusion was at an end. Government itself had lost all public confidence, equally with the bank it had engendered, and which its own arbitrary acts had brought into discredit. "All Paris," says the Regent's mother, in her letters, "has been mourning at the cursed decree which Law has persuaded my son to make. I have received anonymous letters stating that I have nothing to fear on my own account, but that my son shall be pursued with fire and sword."

The Regent now endeavored to avert the odium of his ruinous schemes from himself. He affected to have suddenly lost confidence in Law, and, on the 29th of May, discharged him from his employ as comptroller-general, and stationed a Swiss guard of sixteen men in his house. He even refused to see him, when, on the following day, he applied at the portal of the Palais Royal for admission; but having played off this farce before the public, he admitted him secretly the same night, by a private door, and continued as before to co-operate with him in his financial schemes.

On the first of June, the Regent issued a decree, permitting persons to have as much money as they pleased in their possession. Few, however, were in a state to benefit by this permission. There was a run upon the bank, but a royal ordinance immediately suspended payment, until further orders. To relieve the public mind, a city stock was created, of twenty-five millions, bearing an interest of two and a half per cent, for which bank notes were taken in exchange. The bank notes thus withdrawn from circulation were publicly burned before the Hotel de Ville. The public, however, had lost confidence in everything and everybody, and suspected fraud and collusion in those who pretended to burn the bills.

A general confusion now took place hi the financial world. Families who had lived in opulence found themselves suddenly reduced to indigence. Schemers who had been reveling in the delusion of princely fortune found their estates vanishing into thin air. Those who had any property remaining sought to secure it against reverses. Cautious persons found there was no safety for property in a country where the coin was continually shifting in value, and where a despotism was exercised over public securities, and even over the private purses of individuals. They began to send their effects into other countries; when lo! on the 20th of June a royal edict commanded them to bring back their effects, under penalty of forfeiting twice their value; and forbade them, under like penalty, from investing their money in foreign stocks. This was soon followed by another decree, forbidding any one to retain precious stones in his possession, or to sell them to foreigners; all must be deposited in the bank, in exchange for depreciating paper!

Execrations were now poured out on all sides against Law, and menaces of vengeance. What a contrast, in a short time, to the venal incense that was offered up to him! "This person," writes the Regent's mother, "who was formerly worshiped as a god, is now not sure of his life. It is astonishing how greatly terrified he is. He is as a dead man; he is pale as a sheet, and it is said he can never get over it. My son is not dismayed, though he is threatened on all sides; and is very much amused with Law's terrors."

About the middle of July the last grand attempt was made by Law and the Regent to keep up the system and provide for the immense emission of paper. A decree was fabricated, giving the India Company the entire monopoly of commerce, on condition that it would, in the course of a year, reimburse six hundred millions of livres of its bills, at the rate of fifty millions per month.

On the 17th this decree was sent to parliament to be registered. It at once raised a storm of opposition in that assembly, and a vehement discussion took place. While that was going on a disastrous scene was passing out of doors.

The calamitous effects of the system had reached the humblest concerns of human life. Provisions had risen to an enormous price; paper money was refused at all the shops; the people had not wherewithal to buy bread. It had been found absolutely indispensable to relax a little from the suspension of specie payments, and to allow small sums to be scantily exchanged for paper. The doors of the bank and the neighboring streets were immediately thronged with a famishing multitude, seeking cash for bank notes of ten livres. So great was the press and struggle that several persons were stifled and crushed to death. The mob carried three of the bodies to the courtyard of the Palais Royal. Some cried for the Regent to come forth and behold the effect of his system; others demanded the death of Law, the impostor, who had brought this misery and rum upon the nation.

The moment was critical, the popular fury was rising to a tempest, when Le Blanc, the Secretary of State, stepped forth. He had previously sent for the military, and now only sought to gain tune. Singling out six or seven stout fellows, who seemed to be the ringleaders of the mob: "My good fellows," said he, calmly, "carry away these bodies and place them in some church, and then come back quickly to me for your pay." They immediately obeyed; a kind of funeral procession was formed; the arrival of troops dispersed those who lingered behind; and Paris was probably saved from an insurrection.

About ten o'clock in the morning, all being quiet, Law ventured to go in his carriage to the Palais Royal. He was saluted with cries and curses, as he passed along the streets; and he reached the Palais Royal in a terrible fright. The Regent amused himself with his fears, but retained him with him, and sent off his carriage, which was assailed by the mob, pelted with stones, and the glasses shivered. The news of this outrage was communicated to parliament in the midst of a furious discussion of the decree for the commercial monopoly. The first president, who had been absent for a short time, re-entered, and communicated the tidings in a whimsical couplet:

"Messieurs, Messieurs! bonne nouvelle!

Le carrosse de Law est reduite en carrelle!"

"Gentlemen, Gentlemen! good news!

The carriage of Law is shivered to atoms!"

The members sprang up with joy; "And Law!" exclaimed they, "has he been torn to pieces?" The president was ignorant of the result of the tumult; whereupon the debate was cut short, the decree rejected, and the house adjourned; the members hurrying to learn the particulars. Such was the levity with which public affairs were treated at that dissolute and disastrous period.

On the following day there was an ordinance from the King, prohibiting all popular assemblages; and troops were stationed at various points, and in all public places. The regiment of guards was ordered to hold itself in readiness; and the musketeers to be at their hotels, with their horses ready saddled. A number of small offices were opened, where people might cash small notes, though with great delay and difficulty. An edict was also issued declaring that whoever should refuse to take bank notes in the course of trade should forfeit double the amount!

The continued and vehement opposition of parliament to the whole delusive system of finance had been a constant source of annoyance to the Regent; but this obstinate rejection of his last grand expedient of a commercial monopoly was not to be tolerated. He determined to punish that intractable body. The Abbé Dubois and Law suggested a simple mode; it was to suppress the parliament altogether, being, as they observed, so far from useful that it was a constant impediment to the march of public affairs. The Regent was half inclined to listen to their advice; but upon calmer consideration, and the advice of friends, he adopted a more moderate course. On the 20th of July, early in the morning, all the doors of the parliament-house were taken possession of by troops. Others were sent to surround the house of the first president, and others to the houses of the various members; who were all at first in great alarm, until an order from the King was put into their hands, to render themselves at Pontoise, in the course of two days, to which place the parliament was thus suddenly and arbitrarily transferred.

This despotic act, says Voltaire, would at any other time have caused an insurrection; but one half of the Parisians were occupied by their ruin, and the other half by their fancied riches, which were soon to vanish. The president and members of parliament acquiesced in the mandate without a murmur; they even went as if on a party of pleasure, and made every preparation to lead a joyous life in their exile. The musketeers, who held possession of the vacated parliament-house, a gay corps of fashionable young fellows, amused themselves with making songs and pasquinades, at the expense of the exiled legislators; and at length, to pass away time, formed themselves into a mock parliament; elected their presidents, kings, ministers, and advocates; took their seats in due form, arraigned a cat at their bar, in place of the Sieur Law, and, after giving it a "fair trial," condemned it to be hanged. In this manner public affairs and public institutions were lightly turned to jest.

As to the exiled parliament, it lived gayly and luxuriously at Pontoise, at the public expense; for the Regent had furnished funds, as usual, with a lavish hand. The first president had the mansion of the Duke de Bouillon put at his disposal, already furnished, with a vast and delightful garden on the borders of a river. There he kept open house to all the members of parliament. Several tables were spread every day, all furnished luxuriously and splendidly; the most exquisite wines and liqueurs, the choicest fruits and refreshments, of all kinds, abounded. A number of small chariots for one and two horses were always at hand, for such ladies and old gentlemen as wished to take an airing after dinner, and card and billiard tables for such as chose to amuse themselves in that way until supper. The sister and the daughter of the first president did the honors of the house, and he himself presided there with an air of great ease, hospitality, and magnificence. It became a party of pleasure to drive from Paris to Pontoise, which was six leagues distant, and partake of the amusements and festivities of the place. Business was openly slighted; nothing was thought of but amusement. The regent and his government were laughed at, and made the subjects of continual pleasantries; while the enormous expenses incurred by this idle and lavish course of life more than doubled the liberal sums provided. This was the way in which the parliament resented their exile.

During all this time the system was getting more and more involved. The stock exchange had some time previously been removed to the Place Vendome; but the tumult and noise becoming intolerable to the residents of that polite quarter, and especially to the chancellor, whose hotel was there, the Prince and Princess Carignan, both deep gamblers in Mississippi stock, offered the extensive garden of the Hotel de Soissons as a rallying-place for the worshipers of Mammon. The offer was accepted. A number of barracks were immediately erected in the garden, as offices for the stock-brokers, and an order was obtained from the Regent, under pretext of police regulations, that no bargain should be valid unless concluded in these barracks. The rent of them immediately mounted to a hundred livres a month for each, and the whole yielded these noble proprietors an ignoble revenue of half a million of livres.

The mania for gain, however, was now at an end. A universal panic succeeded. "*Sauve qui peut*!" was the watchword. Every one was anxious to exchange falling paper for something of intrinsic and permanent value. Since money was not to be had, jewels, precious stones, plate, porcelain, trinkets of gold and silver, all commanded any price in paper. Land was bought at fifty years' purchase, and he esteemed himself happy who could get it even at this price. Monopolies now became the rage among the noble holders of paper. The Duke de la Force bought up nearly all the tallow, grease, and soap; others the coffee and spices; others hay and oats. Foreign exchanges were almost impracticable. The debts of Dutch and English merchants were paid in this fictitious money, all the coin of the realm having disappeared. All the relations of debtor and creditor were confounded. With one thousand crowns one might pay a debt of eighteen thousand livres!

The Regent's mother, who once exulted in the affluence of bank paper, now wrote in a very different tone: "I have often wished," said she in her letters, "that these bank-notes were in the depths of the infernal regions. They have given my son more trouble than relief. Nobody in France has a penny . . . My son was once popular, but since the arrival of this cursed Law, he is hated more and more. Not a week passes, without my receiving letters filled with frightful threats, and speaking of him as a tyrant. I have just received one threatening him with poison. When I showed it to him, he did nothing but laugh."

In the meantime, Law was dismayed by the increasing troubles, and terrified at the tempest he had raised. He was not a man of real courage; and fearing for his personal safety, from popular tumult, or the despair of ruined individuals, he again took refuge in the palace of the Regent. The latter, as usual, amused himself with his terrors, and turned every new disaster into a jest; but he too began to think of his own security.

In pursuing the schemes of Law, he had no doubt calculated to carry through his term of government with ease and splendor; and to enrich himself, his connections, and his favorites; and had hoped that the catastrophe of the system would not take place until after the expiration of the regency.

He now saw his mistake; that it was impossible much longer to prevent an explosion; and he determined at once to get Law out of the way, and then to charge him with the whole tissue of delusions of this paper alchemy. He accordingly took occasion of the recall of parliament in December, 1720, to suggest to Law the policy of his avoiding an encounter with that hostile and exasperated body. Law needed no urging to the measure. His only desire was to escape from Paris and its tempestuous populace. Two days before the return of parliament he took his sudden and secret departure. He traveled in a chaise bearing the arms of the Regent, and was escorted by a kind of safeguard of servants in the Duke's livery. His first place of refuge was an estate of the Regent's, about six leagues from Paris, from whence he pushed forward to Bruxelles.

As soon as Law was fairly out of the way, the Duke of Orleans summoned a council of the regency, and informed them that they were assembled to deliberate on the state of the finances, and the affairs of the India Company. Accordingly La Houssaye, Comptroller-General, rendered a perfectly clear statement, by which it appeared that there were bank bills in circulation to the amount of two milliards, seven hundred millions of livres, without any evidence that this enormous sum had been emitted in virtue of any ordinance from the general assembly of the India Company, which alone had the right to authorize such emissions.

The council was astonished at this disclosure, and looked to the Regent for explanation. Pushed to the extreme, the Regent avowed that Law had emitted bills to the amount of twelve hundred millions beyond what had been fixed by ordinances, and in contradiction to express prohibitions; that the thing being done, he, the Regent, had legalized or rather covered the transaction, by decrees ordering such emissions, which decrees he had antedated.

A stormy scene ensued between the Regent and the Duke de Bourbon, little to the credit of either, both having been deeply implicated in the cabalistic operations of the system. In fact, the several members of the council had been among the most venal "beneficiaries" of the scheme, and had interests at stake which they were anxious to secure. From all the circumstances of the case, I am inclined to think that others were more to blame than Law, for the disastrous effects of his financial projects. His bank, had it been confined to its original limits, and left to the control of its own internal regulations, might have gone on prosperously, and been of great benefit to the nation. It was an institution fitted for a free country; but unfortunately it was subjected to the control of a despotic government, that could, at its pleasure, alter the value of the specie within its vaults, and compel the most extravagant expansions of its paper circulation. The vital principle of a bank is security in the regularity of its operations, and the immediate convertibility of its paper into coin; and what confidence could be reposed in an institution or its paper promises, when the sovereign could at any moment centuple those promises in the market, and seize upon all the money in the bank? The compulsory measures used, likewise, to force bank-notes into currency, against the judgment of the public, was fatal to the system; for credit must be free and uncontrolled as the common air. The Regent was the evil spirit of the system, that forced Law on to an expansion of his paper currency far beyond what he had ever dreamed of. He it was that in a manner compelled the unlucky projector to devise all kinds of collateral companies and monopolies, by which to raise funds to meet the constantly and enormously increasing emissions of shares and notes. Law was but like a poor conjurer in the hands of a potent spirit that he has evoked, and that obliges him to go on, desperately and ruinously, with his conjurations. He only thought at the outset to raise the wind, but the Regent compelled him to raise the whirlwind.

The investigation of the affairs of the company by the council resulted in nothing beneficial to the public. The princes and nobles who had enriched themselves by all kinds of juggles and extortions, escaped unpunished, and retained the greater part of their spoils. Many of the "suddenly rich," who had risen from obscurity to a giddy height of imaginary prosperity, and had indulged in all kinds of vulgar and ridiculous excesses, awoke as out of a dream, in their original poverty, now made more galling and humiliating by their transient elevation.

The weight of the evil, however, fell on more valuable classes of society; honest tradesmen and artisans, who had been seduced away from the safe pursuits of industry, to the specious chances of speculation. Thousands of meritorious families also, once opulent, had been reduced to indigence, by a too great confidence in government. There was a general derangement in the finances, that long exerted a baneful influence over the national prosperity; but the most disastrous effects of the system were upon the morals and manners of the nation. The faith of engagements, the sanctity of promises in affairs of business, were at an end. Every expedient to grasp present profit, or to evade present difficulty, was tolerated. While such deplorable laxity of principle was generated in the busy classes, the chivalry of France had soiled their pennons; and honor and glory, so long the idols of the Gallic nobility, had been tumbled to the earth, and trampled in the dirt of the stock-market.

As to Law, the originator of the system, he appears eventually to have profited but little by his schemes. "He was a quack," says Voltaire, "to whom the state was given to be cured, but who poisoned it with his drugs, and who poisoned himself." The effects which he left behind in France were sold at a low price and the proceeds dissipated. His landed estates were confiscated. He carried away with him barely enough to maintain himself, his wife, and daughter, with decency. The chief relic of his immense fortune was a great diamond, which he was often obliged to pawn. He was in England in 1721, and was presented to George the First. He returned shortly afterward to the continent; shifting about from place to place, and died in Venice, in 1729. His wife and daughter, accustomed to live with the prodigality of princesses, could not conform to their altered fortunes, but dissipated the scanty means left to them, and sank into abject poverty. "I saw his wife," says Voltaire, "at Bruxelles, as much humiliated as she had been haughty and triumphant in Paris." An elder brother of Law remained in France, and was protected by the Duchess of Bourbon. His descendants have acquitted themselves honorably, in various public employments; and one of them is the Marquis Lauriston, some time Lieutenant-General and Peer of France.

CHARLES MACKAY

THE MISSISSIPPI SCHEME

from

Memoirs of Extraordinary Popular Delusions and the Madness of Crowds

(1852)

CHARLES MACKAY

THE MISSISSIPPI SCHEME

THE MISSISSIPPI SCHEME

Some in clandestine companies combine;
Erect new stocks to trade beyond the line;
With air and empty names beguile the town,
And raise new credits first, then cry 'em down;
Divide the empty nothing into shares,
And set the crowd together by the ears.

Defoe.

The personal character and career of one man are so intimately connected with the great scheme of the years 1719 and 1720, that a history of the Mississippi madness can have no fitter introduction than a sketch of the life of its great author, John Law. Historians are divided in opinion as to whether they should designate him a knave or a madman. Both epithets were unsparingly applied to him in his lifetime, and while the unhappy consequences of his projects were still deeply felt. Posterity, however, has found reason to doubt the justice of the accusation, and to confess that John Law was neither knave nor madman, but one more deceived than deceiving; more sinned against than sinning. He was thoroughly acquainted with the philosophy and true principles of credit. He understood the monetary question better than any man of his day; and if his system fell with a crash so tremendous, it was not so much his fault as that of the people amongst whom he had erected it. He did not calculate upon the avaricious frenzy of a whole nation; he did not see that confidence, like mistrust, could be increased, almost *ad infinitum*, and that hope was as extravagant as fear. How was he to foretell that the French people, like the man in the fable, would kill, in their frantic eagerness, the fine goose he had brought to lay them so many golden eggs? His fate was like that which may be supposed to have overtaken the first adventurous boatman who rowed from Erie to Ontario. Broad and smooth was the river on which he embarked; rapid and pleasant was his progress; and who was to stay him in his career? Alas for him! the cataract was nigh. He saw, when it was too late, that the tide which wafted him so joyously along was a tide of destruction; and when he endeavoured to retrace his way, he found that the current was too strong for his weak efforts to stem, and that he drew nearer every instant to the tremendous falls. Down he went over the sharp rocks, and the waters with him. He was dashed to pieces with his bark, but the waters, maddened and turned to foam by the rough descent, only boiled and bubbled for a time, and then flowed on again as smoothly as ever. Just so it was with Law and the French people. He was the boatman and they were the waters.

John Law was born at Edinburgh in the year 1671. His father was the younger son of an ancient family in Fife, and carried on the business of a goldsmith and banker. He amassed considerable wealth in his trade, sufficient to enable him to gratify the wish, so common among his countrymen, of adding a territorial designation to his name. He purchased with this view the estates of Lauriston and Randleston, on the Frith of Forth on the borders of West and Mid Lothian, and was thenceforth known as Law of Lauriston. The subject of our memoir, being the eldest son, was received into his father's counting-house at the age of fourteen, and for three years laboured hard to acquire an insight into the principles of banking, as then carried on in Scotland. He had always manifested great love for the study of numbers, and his proficiency in the mathematics was considered extraordinary in one of his tender years. At the age of seventeen he was tall, strong, and well made; and his face, although deeply scarred with the small-pox, was agreeable in its expression, and full of intelligence. At this time he began to neglect his business, and becoming vain of his person, indulged in considerable extravagance of attire. He was a great favourite with the ladies, by whom he was called Beau Law, while the other sex, despising his foppery, nicknamed him Jessamy John. At the death of his father, which happened in 1688, he withdrew entirely from the desk, which had become so irksome, and being possessed of the revenues of the paternal estate of Lauriston, he proceeded to London, to see the world.

He was now very young, very vain, good-looking, tolerably rich, and quite uncontrolled. It is no wonder that, on his arrival in the capital, he should launch out into extravagance. He soon became a regular frequenter of the gaming-houses, and by pursuing a certain plan, based upon some abstruse calculation of chances, he contrived to gain considerable sums. All the gamblers envied him his luck, and many made it a point to watch his play, and stake their money on the same chances. In affairs of gallantry he was equally fortunate; ladies of the first rank smiled graciously upon the handsome Scotchman – the young, the rich, the witty, and the obliging. But all these successes only paved the way for reverses. After he had been for nine years exposed to the dangerous attractions of the gay life he was leading, he became an irrecoverable gambler. As his love of play increased in violence, it diminished in prudence.

Great losses were only to be repaired by still greater ventures, and one unhappy day he lost more than he could repay without mortgaging his family estate. To that step he was driven at last. At the same time his gallantry brought him into trouble. A love affair, or slight flirtation, with a lady of the name of Villiers [1] exposed him to the resentment of a Mr. Wilson, by whom he was challenged to fight a duel. Law accepted, and had the ill fortune to shoot his antagonist dead upon the spot. He was arrested the same day, and brought to trial for murder by the relatives of Mr. Wilson. He was afterwards found guilty, and sentenced to death. The sentence was commuted to a fine, upon the ground that the offence only amounted to manslaughter. An appeal being lodged by a brother of the deceased, Law was detained in the King's Bench, whence, by some means or other, which he never explained, he contrived to escape; and an action being instituted against the sheriffs, he was advertised in the Gazette, and a reward offered for his apprehension. He was described as "Captain John Law, a Scotchman, aged twenty-six; a very tall, black, lean man; well shaped, above six feet high, with large pock-holes in his face; big nosed, and speaking broad and loud." As this was rather a caricature than a description of him, it has been supposed that it was drawn up with a view to favour his escape. He succeeded in reaching the Continent, where he travelled for three years, and devoted much of his attention to the monetary and banking affairs of the countries through which he passed. He stayed a few months in Amsterdam, and speculated to some extent in the funds. His mornings were devoted to the study of finance and the principles of trade, and his evenings to the gaming-house. It is generally believed that he returned to Edinburgh in the year 1700. It is certain that he published in that city his "Proposals and Reasons for constituting a Council of Trade." This pamphlet did not excite

1. Miss Elizabeth Villiers, afterwards Countess of Orkney.

much attention.

In a short time afterwards he published a project for establishing what he called a Land-bank,[2] the notes issued by which were never to exceed the value of the entire lands of the state, upon ordinary interest, or were to be equal in value to the land, with the right to enter into possession at a certain time. The project excited a good deal of discussion in the Scottish parliament, and a motion for the establishment of such a bank was brought forward by a neutral party, called the Squadrone, whom Law had interested in his favour. The Parliament ultimately passed a resolution to the effect, that, to establish any kind of paper credit, so as to force it to pass, was an improper expedient for the nation.

Upon the failure of this project, and of his efforts to procure a pardon for the murder of Mr. Wilson, Law withdrew to the Continent, and resumed his old habits of gaming. For fourteen years he continued to roam about, in Flanders, Holland, Germany, Hungary, Italy, and France. He soon became intimately acquainted with the extent of the trade and resources of each, and daily more confirmed in his opinion that no country could prosper without a paper currency. During the whole of this time he appears to have chiefly supported himself by successful play. At every gambling-house of note in the capitals of Europe, he was known and appreciated as one better skilled in the intricacies of chance than any other man of the day. It is stated in the *Biographie Universelle* that he was expelled, first from Venice, and afterwards from Genoa, by the magistrates, who thought him a visitor too dangerous for the youth of those cities. During his residence in Paris he rendered himself obnoxious to D'Argenson, the lieutenant-general of the police, by whom he was ordered to quit the capital. This did

2. The wits of the day called it a sand-bank, which would wreck the vessel of the state.

not take place, however, before he had made the acquaintance in the saloons, of the Duke de Vendôme, the Prince de Conti, and of the gay Duke of Orleans, the latter of whom was destined afterwards to exercise so much influence over his fate. The Duke of Orleans was pleased with the vivacity and good sense of the Scottish adventurer, while the latter was no less pleased with the wit and amiability of a prince who promised to become his patron. They were often thrown into each other's society, and Law seized every opportunity to instil his financial doctrines into the mind of one whose proximity to the throne pointed him out as destined, at no very distant date, to play an important part in the government.

Shortly before the death of Louis XIV, or, as some say, in 1708, Law proposed a scheme of finance to Desmarets, the Comptroller. Louis is reported to have inquired whether the projector were a Catholic, and, on being answered in the negative, to have declined having anything to do with him.[3]

It was after this repulse that he visited Italy. His mind being still occupied with schemes of finance, he proposed to Victor Amadeus, Duke of Savoy, to establish his land-bank in that country. The Duke replied that his dominions were too circumscribed for the execution of so great a project, and that he was by far too poor a potentate to be ruined. He advised him, however, to try the King of France once more; for he was sure, if he knew anything of the French character, that the people would be delighted with a plan, not only so new, but

3. This anecdote, which is related in the correspondence of Madame de Baviere, Duchess of Orleans, and mother of the Regent, is discredited by Lord John Russell, in his "History of the principal States of Europe, from the Peace of Utrecht;" for what reason he does not inform us. There is no doubt that Law proposed his scheme to Desmarets, and that Louis refused to hear of it. The reason given for the refusal is quite consistent with the character of that bigoted and tyrannical monarch.

so plausible.

Louis XIV died in 1715, and the heir to the throne being an infant only seven years of age, the Duke of Orleans assumed the reins of government, as Regent, during his minority. Law now found himself in a more favourable position. The tide in his affairs had come, which, taken at the flood, was to waft him on to fortune. The Regent was his friend, already acquainted with his theory and pretensions, and inclined, moreover, to aid him in any efforts to restore the wounded credit of France, bowed down to the earth by the extravagance of the long reign of Louis XIV.

Hardly was that monarch laid in his grave ere the popular hatred, suppressed so long, burst forth against his memory. He who, during his life, had been flattered with an excess of adulation, to which history scarcely offers a parallel, was now cursed as a tyrant, a bigot, and a plunderer. His statues were pelted and disfigured; his effigies torn down, amid the execrations of the populace, and his name rendered synonymous with selfishness and oppression. The glory of his arms was forgotten, and nothing was remembered but his reverses, his extravagance, and his cruelty.

The finances of the country were in a state of the utmost disorder. A profuse and corrupt monarch, whose profuseness and corruption were imitated by almost every functionary, from the highest to the lowest grade, had brought France to the verge of ruin. The national debt amounted to 3000 millions of livres, the revenue to 145 millions, and the expenditure to 142 millions per annum; leaving only three millions to pay the interest upon 3000 millions. The first care of the Regent was to discover a remedy for an evil of such magnitude, and a council was early summoned to take the matter into consideration. The Duke de St. Simon was of opinion that nothing could save the country from revolution but a remedy at once bold and dangerous. He advised the Regent to convoke the States-General, and declare a national bankruptcy. The Duke de Noailles, a man of accommodating principles, an accomplished courtier, and totally averse from giving himself any trouble or annoyance that ingenuity could escape from, opposed the project of St. Simon with all his influence. He represented the expedient as alike dishonest and ruinous. The Regent was of the same opinion, and this desperate remedy fell to the ground.

The measures ultimately adopted, though they promised fair, only aggravated the evil. The first, and most dishonest measure, was of no advantage to the state. A recoinage was ordered, by which the currency was depreciated one-fifth; those who took a thousand pieces of gold or silver to the mint received back an amount of coin of the same nominal value, but only four-fifths of the weight of metal. By this contrivance the treasury gained seventy-two millions of livres, and all the commercial operations of the country were disordered. A trifling diminution of the taxes silenced the clamours of the people, and for the slight present advantage the great prospective evil was forgotten.

A chamber of justice was next instituted, to inquire into the malversations of the loan-contractors and the farmers of the revenues. Tax collectors are never very popular in any country, but those of France at this period deserved all the odium with which they were loaded. As soon as these farmers-general, with all their hosts of subordinate agents, called *maltotiers*,[4] were called to account for their misdeeds, the most extravagant joy took possession of the nation. The Chamber of Justice, instituted chiefly for this purpose, was endowed with very extensive powers. It was composed of the presidents and councils of the parliament, the judges of the Courts of Aid and of Requests, and the officers of the Chamber of Account, under

4. From *maltôte*, an oppressive tax.

the general presidence of the minister of finance. Informers were encouraged to give evidence against the offenders by the promise of one-fifth part of the fines and confiscations. A tenth of all concealed effects belonging to the guilty was promised to such as should furnish the means of discovering them.

The promulgation of the edict constituting this court caused a degree of consternation among those principally concerned which can only be accounted for on the supposition that their peculation had been enormous. But they met with no sympathy. The proceedings against them justified their terror. The Bastile was soon unable to contain the prisoners that were sent to it, and the gaols all over the country teemed with guilty or suspected persons. An order was issued to all innkeepers and postmasters to refuse horses to such as endeavoured to seek safety in flight; and all persons were forbidden, under heavy fines, to harbour them or favour their evasion. Some were condemned to the pillory, others to the gallies, and the least guilty to fine and imprisonment. One only, Samuel Bernard, a rich banker, and farmer-general of a province remote from the capital, was sentenced to death. So great had been the illegal profits of this man, -- looked upon as the tyrant and oppressor of his district, -- that he offered six millions of livres, or 250,000*l.* sterling, to be allowed to escape.

His bribe was refused, and he suffered the penalty of death. Others, perhaps more guilty, were more fortunate. Confiscation, owing to the concealment of their treasures by the delinquents, often produced less money than a fine. The severity of the government relaxed, and fines, under the denomination of taxes, were indiscriminately levied upon all offenders. But so corrupt was every department of the administration, that the country benefited but little by the sums which thus flowed into the treasury. Courtiers, and courtiers' wives and mistresses, came in for the chief share of the spoils. One contractor had been taxed in proportion to his wealth and guilt, at the sum of twelve millions of livres. The Count * * *, a man of some weight in the government, called upon him, and offered to procure a remission of the fine, if he would give him a hundred thousand crowns. "Vous êtes trop tard, mon ami," replied the financier; "I have already made a bargain with your wife for fifty thousand."[5]

About a hundred and eighty millions of livres were levied in this manner, of which eighty were applied in payment of the debts contracted by the government. The remainder found its way into the pockets of the courtiers. Madame de Maintenon, writing on this subject, says, "We hear every day of some new grant of the Regent; the people murmur very much at this mode of employing the money taken from the peculators." The people, who, after the first burst of their resentment is over, generally express a sympathy for the weak, were indignant that so much severity should be used to so little purpose. They did not see the justice of robbing one set of rogues to fatten another. In a few months all the more guilty had been brought to punishment, and the chamber of justice looked for victims in humbler walks of life. Charges of fraud and extortion were brought against tradesmen of good character, in consequence of the great inducements held out to common informers. They were compelled to lay open their affairs before this tribunal in order to establish their innocence. The voice of complaint resounded from every side, and at the expiration of a year

5. This anecdote is related by M. de la Hode, in his Life of Philippe of Orleans. It would have looked more authentic if he had given the names of the dishonest contractor and the still more dishonest minister. But M. de la Hode's book is liable to the same objection as most of the French memoirs of that and of subsequent periods. It is sufficient with most of them that an anecdote be *ben trovato*; the *vero* is but matter of secondary consideration.

the government found it advisable to discontinue further proceedings. The chamber of justice was suppressed, and a general amnesty granted to all against whom no charges had yet been preferred.

In the midst of this financial confusion Law appeared upon the scene. No man felt more deeply than the Regent the deplorable state of the country, but no man could be more averse from putting his shoulders manfully to the wheel. He disliked business; he signed official documents without proper examination, and trusted to others what he should have undertaken himself. The cares inseparable from his high office were burdensome to him; he saw that something was necessary to be done, but he lacked the energy to do it, and had not virtue enough to sacrifice his case and his pleasures in the attempt. No wonder that, with this character, he listened favourably to the mighty projects, so easy of execution, of the clever adventurer whom he had formerly known, and whose talents he appreciated.

When Law presented himself at court, he was most cordially received. He offered two memorials to the Regent, in which he set forth the evils that had befallen France, owing to an insufficient currency, at different times depreciated. He asserted that a metallic currency, unaided by a paper money, was wholly inadequate to the wants of a commercial country, and particularly cited the examples of Great Britain and Holland to show the advantages of paper. He used many sound arguments on the subject of credit, and proposed, as a means of restoring that of France, then at so low an ebb among the nations, that he should be allowed to set up a bank, which should have the management of the royal revenues, and issue notes, both on that and on landed security. He further proposed that this bank should be administered in the King's name, but subject to the control of commissioners, to be named by the States-General.

While these memorials were under consideration, Law translated into French his essay on money and trade, and used every means to extend through the nation his renown as a financier. He soon became talked of. The confidants of the Regent spread abroad his praise, and every one expected great things of Monsieur Lass.[6]

On the 5th of May, 1716, a royal edict was published, by which Law was authorised, in conjunction with his brother, to establish a bank, under the name of Law and Company, the notes of which should be received in payment of the taxes. The capital was fixed at six millions of livres, in twelve thousand shares of five hundred livres each, purchasable one-fourth in specie and the remainder in *billets d'état*. It was not thought expedient to grant him the whole of the privileges prayed for in his memorials until experience should have shown their safety and advantage.

Law was now on the high road to fortune. The study of thirty years was brought to guide him in the management of his bank. He made all his notes payable at sight, and in the coin current at the time they were issued. This last was a master-stroke of policy, and immediately rendered his notes more valuable than the precious metals. The latter were constantly liable to depreciation by the unwise tampering of the government. A thousand livres of silver might be worth their nominal value one day and be reduced one-sixth the next, but a note of Law's bank retained its original value. He publicly declared at the same time that a banker deserved death if he made issues without having sufficient security to answer all demands. The consequence was, that his notes advanced rapidly in public

---

6. The French pronounced his name in this manner to avoid the ungallic sound, *aw*. After the failure of his scheme, the wags said the nation was *lasse de lui*, and proposed that he should in future be known by the name of Monsieur *Helas*!

estimation, and were received at one per cent. more than specie. It was not long before the trade of the country felt the benefit. Languishing commerce began to lift up her head; the taxes were paid with greater regularity and less murmuring, and a degree of confidence was established that could not fail, if it continued, to become still more advantageous. In the course of a year Law's notes rose to fifteen per cent. premium, while the *billets d'état*, or notes issued by the government, as security fort he debts contracted by the extravagant Louis XIV, were at a discount of no less than seventy-eight and a half per cent. The comparison was too great in favour of Law not to attract the attention of the whole kingdom, and his credit extended itself day by day. Branches of his bank were almost simultaneously established at Lyons, Rochelle, Tours, Amiens, and Orleans.

The Regent appears to have been utterly astonished at his success, and gradually to have conceived the idea, that paper, which could so aid a metallic currency, could entirely supersede it. Upon this fundamental error he afterwards acted. In the mean time, Law commenced the famous project which has handed his name down to posterity. He proposed to the Regent, who could refuse him nothing, to establish a company, that should have the exclusive privilege of trading to the great river Mississippi and the province of Louisiana, on its western bank. The country was supposed to abound in the precious metals, and the company, supported by the profits of their exclusive commerce, were to be the sole farmers of the taxes, and sole coiners of money. Letters patent were issued, incorporating the company, in August 1717. The capital was divided into two hundred thousand shares of five hundred livres each, the whole of which might be paid in *billets d'état*, at their nominal value, although worth no more than 160 livres in the market.

It was now that the frenzy of speculating began to seize upon the nation. Law's bank had effected so much good, that any promises for the future which he thought proper to make were readily believed. The Regent every day conferred new privileges upon the fortunate projector. The bank obtained the monopoly of the sale of tobacco; the sole right of refinage of gold and silver, and was finally erected into the Royal Bank of France. Amid the intoxication of success, both Law and the Regent forgot the maxim so loudly proclaimed by the former, that a banker deserved death who made issues of paper without the necessary funds to provide for them. As soon as the bank, from a private, became a public institution, the Regent caused a fabrication of notes to the amount of one thousand millions of livres. This was the first departure from sound principles, and one for which Law is not justly blameable. While the affairs of the bank were under his control, the issues had never exceeded sixty millions. Whether Law opposed the inordinate increase is not known, but as it took place as soon as the bank was made a royal establishment, it is but fair to lay the blame of the change of system upon the Regent.

Law found that he lived under a despotic government, but he was not yet aware of the pernicious influence which such a government could exercise upon so delicate a framework as that of credit. He discovered it afterwards to his cost, but in the mean time suffered himself to be impelled by the Regent into courses which his own reason must have disapproved. With a weakness most culpable, he lent his aid in inundating the country with paper money, which, based upon no solid foundation, was sure to fall, sooner or later. The extraordinary present fortune dazzled his eyes, and prevented him from seeing the evil day that would burst over his head, when once, from any cause or other, the alarm was sounded. The Parliament were from the first jealous of his influence as a foreigner, and had, besides, their misgivings as to the safety of his projects. As his influence extended, their animosity increased. D'Aguesseau, the Chancellor, was unceremoniously dismissed by the Regent for his opposition to the vast increase of paper money, and the constant depreciation of the gold and silver coin of the realm. This only served to augment the enmity of the Parliament, and when D'Argenson, a man devoted to the interests of the Regent, was appointed to the vacant chancellorship, and made at the same time minister of finance, they became more violent than ever. The first measure of the new minister caused a further depreciation of the coin. In order to extinguish the *billets d'état*, it was ordered that persons bringing to the mint four thousand livres in specie and one thousand livres in billets d'État, should receive back coin to the amount of five thousand livres. D'Argenson plumed himself mightily upon thus creating five thousand new and smaller livres out of the four thousand old and larger ones, being too ignorant of the true principles of trade and credit to be aware of the immense injury he was inflicting upon both.

The Parliament saw at once the impolicy and danger of such a system, and made repeated remonstrances to the Regent. The latter refused to entertain their petitions, when the Parliament, by a bold, and very unusual stretch of authority, commanded that no money should be received in payment but that of the old standard. The Regent summoned a *lit de justice*, and annulled the decree. The Parliament resisted, and issued another. Again the Regent exercised his privilege, and annulled it, till the Parliament, stung to fiercer opposition, passed another decree, dated August 12th, 1718, by which they forbade the bank of Law to have any concern, either direct or indirect, in the administration of the revenue; and prohibited all foreigners, under heavy penalties, from interfering, either in their own names, or in that of others, in the management of the finances of the state. The Parliament considered Law to be the author of all the evil, and some of the counsellors, in the virulence of their enmity, proposed that he should be brought to trial, and, if found guilty, be hung at the gates of the Palais de Justice.

Law, in great alarm, fled to the Palais Royal, and threw himself on the protection of the Regent, praying that measures might be taken to reduce the Parliament to obedience. The Regent had nothing so much at heart, both on that account and because of the disputes that had arisen relative to the legitimation of the Duke of Maine and the Count of Thoulouse, the sons of the late King. The Parliament was ultimately overawed by the arrest of their president and two of the counsellors, who were sent to distant prisons.

Thus the first cloud upon Law's prospects blew over: freed from apprehension of personal danger, he devoted his attention to his famous Mississippi project, the shares of which were rapidly rising, in spite of the Parliament. At the commencement of the year 1719 an edict was published, granting to the Mississippi Company the exclusive privilege of trading to the East Indies, China, and the South Seas, and to all the possessions of the French East India Company, established by Colbert. The Company, in consequence of this great increase of their business, assumed, as more appropriate, the title of Company of the Indies, and created fifty thousand new shares. The prospects now held out by Law were most magnificent. He promised a yearly dividend of two hundred livres upon each share of five hundred, which, as the shares were paid for in *billets d'État*, at their nominal value, but worth only 100 livres, was at the rate of about 120 percent. profit.

The public enthusiasm, which had been so long rising, could not resist a vision so splendid. At least three hundred thousand applications were made for the fifty thousand new shares, and Law's house in the Rue de Quincampoix was beset from morning to night by the eager applicants. As it was impossible to satisfy them all, it was several weeks before a list of the fortunate new stockholders could be made out, during which time the public impatience rose to a pitch of frenzy. Dukes, marquises, counts, with their duchesses, marchionesses, and countesses, waited in the streets for hours every day before Mr. Law's door to know the result. At last, to avoid the jostling of the plebeian crowd, which, to the number of thousands, filled the whole thoroughfare, they took apartments in the adjoining houses, that they might be continually near the temple whence the new Plutus was diffusing wealth. Every day the value of the old shares increased, and the fresh applications, induced by the golden dreams of the whole nation, became so numerous that it was deemed advisable to create no less than three hundred thousand new shares, at five thousand livres each, in order that the Regent might take advantage of the popular enthusiasm to pay off the national debt. For this purpose, the sum of fifteen hundred millions of livres was necessary. Such was the eagerness of the nation, that thrice the sum would have been subscribed if the government had authorised it.

Law was now at the zenith of his prosperity, and the people were rapidly approaching the zenith of their infatuation. The highest and the lowest classes were alike filled with a vision of boundless wealth. There was not a person of note among the aristocracy, with the exception of the Duke of St. Simon and Marshal Villars, who was not engaged in buying or selling stock. People of every age and sex, and condition in life, speculated in the rise and fall of the Mississippi bonds. The Rue de Quincampoix was the grand resort of the jobbers, and it being a narrow, inconvenient street, accidents continually occurred in it, from the tremendous pressure of the crowd. Houses in it, worth, in ordinary times, a thousand livres of yearly rent, yielded as much as twelve or sixteen thousand. A cobbler, who had a stall in it, gained about two hundred livres a day by letting it out, and furnishing writing materials to brokers and their clients. The story goes, that a hump-backed man who stood in the street gained considerable sums by lending his hump as a writing-desk to the eager speculators! The great concourse of persons who assembled to do business brought a still greater concourse of spectators. These again drew all the thieves and immoral characters of Paris to the spot, and constant riots and disturbances took place. At nightfall, it was often found necessary to send a troop of soldiers to clear the street.

Law, finding the inconvenience of his residence, removed to the Place Vendôme, whither the crowd of *agioteurs* followed him. That spacious square soon became as thronged as the Rue de Quincampoix: from morning to night it presented the appearance of a fair. Booths and tents were erected for the transaction of business and the sale of refreshments, and gamblers with their roulette tables stationed themselves in the very middle of the place, and reaped a golden, or rather a paper, harvest from the throng. The Boulevards and public gardens were forsaken; parties of pleasure took their walks in preference in the Place Vendôme, which became the fashionable lounge of the idle, as well as the general rendezvous of the busy. The noise was so great all day, that the Chancellor, whose court was situated in the square, complained to the Regent and the municipality, that he could not hear the advocates. Law, when applied to, expressed his willingness to aid in the removal of the nuisance, and for this purpose entered into a treaty with the Prince de Carignan for the Hôtel de Soissons, which had a garden of several acres in the rear. A bargain was concluded, by which Law became the purchaser of the hotel, at an enormous price, the Prince reserving to himself the magnificent gardens as a new source of profit. They contained some fine statues and several fountains, and were altogether laid out with much taste. As soon as Law was installed in his new abode, an edict was published, forbidding all persons to buy or sell stock anywhere but in the gardens of the Hôtel de Soissons. In the midst among the trees, about five hundred small tents and pavilions were erected, for the convenience of the stock-jobbers. Their various colours, the gay ribands and banners which floated from them, the busy crowds which passed continually in and out, the incessant hum of voices, the noise, the music, and the strange mixture of business and pleasure on the countenances of the throng, all combined to give the place an air of enchantment that quite enraptured the Parisians. The Prince de Carignan made enormous profits while the delusion lasted. Each tent was let at the rate of five hundred livres a month; and, as there were at least five hundred of them, his monthly revenue from this source alone must have amounted to 250,000 livres, or upwards of 10,000*l* sterling.

The honest old soldier, Marshal Villars, was so vexed to see the folly which had smitten his countrymen, that he never could speak with temper on the subject. Passing one day through the Place Vendôme in his carriage, the choleric gentleman was so annoyed at the infatuation of the people, that he abruptly ordered his coachman to stop, and, putting his head out of the carriage window, harangued them for full half an hour on their "disgusting avarice." This was not a very wise proceeding on his part. Hisses and shouts of laughter resounded from every side, and jokes without number were aimed at him. There being at last strong symptoms that something more tangible was flying through the air in the direction of his head, Marshal was glad to drive on. He never again repeated the experiment.

Two sober, quiet, and philosophic men of letters, M. de la Motte and the Abbé Terrason, congratulated each other, that they, at least, were free from this strange infatuation. A few days afterwards, as the worthy Abbé was coming out of the Hôtel de Soissons, whither he had gone to buy shares in the Mississippi, whom should he see but his friend La Motte entering for the same purpose. "Ha!" said the Abbé, smiling, "is that you?" "Yes," said La Motte, pushing past him as fast as he was able; "and can that be you?" The next time the two scholars met, they talked of philosophy, of science, and of religion, but neither had courage for a long time to breathe one syllable about the Mississippi. At last, when it was mentioned, they agreed that a man ought never to swear against his doing any one thing, and that there was no sort of extravagance of which even a wise man was not capable.

During this time, Law, the new Plutus, had become all at once the most important personage of the state. The ante-chambers of the Regent were forsaken by the courtiers. Peers, judges, and bishops thronged to the Hôtel de Soissons; officers of the army and navy, ladies of title and fashion, and every one to whom hereditary rank or public employ gave a claim to precedence, were to be found waiting in his ante-chambers to beg for a portion of his India stock. Law was so pestered that he was unable to see one-tenth part of the applicants, and every manoeuvre that ingenuity could suggest was employed to gain access to him. Peers, whose dignity would have been outraged if the Regent had made them wait half an hour for an interview, were content to wait six hours for the chance of seeing Monsieur Law. Enormous fees were paid to his servants, if they would merely announce their names. Ladies of rank employed the blandishments of their smiles for the same object; but many of them came day after day for a fortnight before they could obtain an audience. When Law accepted an invitation, he was sometimes so surrounded by ladies, all asking to have their names putdown in his lists as shareholders in the new stock, that, in spite of his well-known and habitual gallantry, he was obliged to tear himself away *par force*. The most ludicrous stratagems were employed to have an opportunity of speaking to him. One lady, who had striven in vain during several days, gave up in despair all attempts to see him at his own house, but ordered her coachman to keep a strict watch whenever she was out in her carriage, and if he saw Mr. Law coming, to drive against a post, and upset her. The coachman promised obedience, and for three days the lady was driven incessantly through the town, praying inwardly for the opportunity to be overturned. At last she espied Mr. Law, and, pulling the string, called out to the coachman, "Upset us now! for God's sake, upset us now!" The coachman drove against a post, the lady screamed, the coach was overturned, and Law, who had seen the accident, hastened to the spot to render assistance. The cunning dame was led into the Hôtel de Soissons, where she soon thought it advisable to recover from her fright, and, after apologizing to Mr. Law, confessed her stratagem. Law smiled, and entered the lady in his books as the purchaser of a quantity of India stock. Another story is told of a Madame de Boucha, who, knowing that Mr. Law was at dinner at a certain house, proceeded thither in her carriage, and gave the alarm of fire. The company started from table, and Law among the rest; but, seeing one lady making all haste into the house towards him, while everybody else was scampering away, he suspected the trick, and ran off in another direction.

Many other anecdotes are related, which even, though they may be a little exaggerated, are nevertheless worth preserving, as showing the spirit of that singular period.[7] The Regent was one day mentioning, in the presence of D'Argenson, the Abbé Dubois, and some other persons, that he was desirous

7. The curious reader may find an anecdote of the eagerness of the French ladies to retain Law in their company, which will make him blush or smile according as he happens to be very modest or the reverse. It is related in the Letters of Madame Charlotte Elizabeth de Bavière, Duchess of Orleans, vol. ii. p. 274.

of deputing some lady, of the rank at least of a Duchess, to attend upon his daughter at Modena; "but," added he, "I do not exactly know where to find one." "No!" replied one, in affected surprise; "I can tell you where to find every Duchess in France: you have only to go to Mr. Law's; you will see them every one in his ante-chamber."

M. de Chirac, a celebrated physician, had bought stock at an unlucky period, and was very anxious to sell out. Stock, however continued to fall for two or three days, much to his alarm. His mind was filled with the subject, when he was suddenly called upon to attend a lady, who imagined herself unwell. He arrived, was shown upstairs, and felt the lady's pulse. "It falls! it falls! good God! it falls continually!" said he, musingly, while the lady looked up in his face, all anxiety for his opinion. "Oh! M. de Chirac," said she, starting to her feet, and ringing the bell for assistance; "I am dying! I am dying! it falls! it falls! it falls!" "What falls?" inquired the doctor, in amazement. "My pulse! my pulse!" said the lady; "I must be dying." "Calm your apprehensions, my dear Madam," said M. de Chirac; "I was speaking of the stocks. The truth is, I have been a great loser, and my mind is so disturbed, I hardly know what I have been saying."

The price of shares sometimes rose ten or twenty per cent. in the course of a few hours, and many persons in the humbler walks of life, who had risen poor in the morning, went to bed in affluence. An extensive holder of stock, being taken ill, sent his servant to sell two hundred and fifty shares, at eight thousand livres each, the price at which they were then quoted. The servant went, and, on his arrival in the Jardin de Soissons, found that in the interval the price had risen to ten thousand livres. The difference of two thousand livres on the two hundred and fifty shares, amounting to 500,000 livres, or 20,000*l* sterling, he very coolly transferred to his own use, and, giving the remainder to his master, set out the same evening for another country. Law's coachman in a very short time made money enough to set up a carriage of his own, and requested permission to leave his service. Law, who esteemed the man, begged of him as a favour, that he would endeavour, before he went, to find a substitute as good as himself. The coachman consented, and in the evening brought two of his former comrades, telling Mr. Law to choose between them, and he would take the other. Cook-maids and footmen were now and then as lucky, and, in the full-blown pride of their easily-acquired wealth, made the most ridiculous mistakes. Preserving the language and manners of their old, with the finery of their new station, they afforded continual subjects for the pity of the sensible, the contempt of the sober, and the laughter of everybody. But the folly and meanness of the higher ranks of society were still more disgusting. One instance alone, related by the Duke de St. Simon, will show the unworthy avarice which infected the whole of society. A man of the name of André, without character or education, had, by a series of well-timed speculations in Mississippi bonds, gained enormous wealth, in an incredibly short space of time. As St. Simon expresses it, "he had amassed mountains of gold." As he became rich, he grew ashamed of the lowness of his birth, and anxious above all things to be allied to nobility. He had a daughter, an infant only three years of age, and he opened a negotiation with the aristocratic and needy family of D'Oyse, that this child should, upon certain conditions, marry a member of that house. The Marquis d'Oyse, to his shame, consented, and promised to marry her himself on her attaining the age of twelve, if the father would pay him down the sum of a hundred thousand crowns, and twenty thousand livres every year, until the celebration of the marriage. The Marquis was himself in his thirty-third year. This scandalous bargain was duly signed and sealed, the stockjobber furthermore agreeing to settle upon his daughter, on the marriage-day, a fortune of several millions. The Duke of Brancas, the head of the family, was present throughout the negotiation, and shared in all the profits. St. Simon, who treats the matter with the levity becoming what he thought so good a joke, adds, "that people did not spare their animadversions on this beautiful marriage," and further informs us, "that the project fell to the ground some months afterwards by the overthrow of Law, and the ruin of the ambitious Monsieur André." It would appear, however, that the noble family never had the honesty to return the hundred thousand crowns.

Amid events like these, which, humiliating though they be, partake largely of the ludicrous, others occurred of a more serious nature. Robberies in the streets were of daily occurrence, in consequence of the immense sums, in paper, which people carried about with them. Assassinations were also frequent. One case in particular fixed the attention of the whole of France, not only on account of the enormity of the offence, but of the rank and high connexions of the criminal.

The Count d'Horn, a younger brother of the Prince d'Horn, and related to the noble families of D'Aremberg, De Ligne, and De Montmorency, was a young man of dissipated character, extravagant to a degree, and unprincipled as he was extravagant. In connexion with two other young men as reckless as himself, named Mille, a Piedmontese captain, and one Destampes, or Lestang, a Fleming, he formed a design to rob a very rich broker, who was known, unfortunately for himself, to carry great sums about his person. The Count pretended a desire to purchase of him a number of shares in the Company of the Indies, and for that purpose appointed to meet him in a *cabaret*, or low public-house, in the neighbourhood of the Place Vendôme. The unsuspecting broker was punctual to his appointment; so were the Count d'Horn and his two associates, whom he introduced as his particular friends. After a few moments' conversation, the Count d'Horn suddenly sprang upon his victim, and stabbed him three times in the breast with a poniard. The man fell heavily to the ground, and, while the Count was employed in rifling his portfolio of bonds in the Mississippi and Indian schemes to the amount of one hundred thousand crowns, Mille, the Piedmontese, stabbed the unfortunate broker again and again, to make sure of his death. But the broker did not fall without a struggle, and his cries brought the people of the *cabaret* to his assistance. Lestang, the other assassin, who had been set to keep watch at a staircase, sprang from a window and escaped; but Mille and the Count d'Horn were seized in the very act.

This crime, committed in open day, and in so public a place as a *cabaret*, filled Paris with consternation. The trial of the assassins commenced on the following day, and the evidence being so clear, they were both found guilty and condemned to be broken alive on the wheel. The noble relatives of the Count d'Horn absolutely blocked up the ante-chambers of the Regent, praying for mercy on the misguided youth, and alleging that he was insane. The Regent avoided them as long as possible, being determined that, in a case so atrocious, justice should take its course; but the importunity of these influential suitors was not to be overcome so silently, and they at last forced themselves into the presence of the Regent, and prayed him to save their house the shame of a public execution. They hinted that the Princes d'Horn were allied to the illustrious family of Orleans, and added that the Regent himself would be disgraced if a kinsman of his should die by the hands of a common executioner. The Regent, to his credit, was proof against all their solicitations, and replied to their last argument in the words of Corneille,-

"Le crime fait la honte, et non pas l'échafaud:"

adding, that whatever shame there might be in the punishment he would very willingly share with the other relatives. Day after day they renewed their entreaties, but always with the same result. At last they thought that if they could interest the Duke de St. Simon intheir layout, a man for whom the Regent felt sincere esteem, they might succeed in their object. The Duke, a thorough aristocrat, was as shocked as they were, that a noble assassin should die by the same death as a plebeian felon, and represented to the Regent the impolicy of making enemies of so numerous, wealthy, and powerful a family. He urged, too, that in Germany, where the family of D'Aremberg had large possessions, it was the law, that no relative of a person broken on the wheel could succeed to any public office or employ until a whole generation had passed away. For this reason he thought the punishment of the guilty Count might be transmuted into beheading, which was considered all over Europe as much less infamous. The Regent was moved by this argument, and was about to consent, when Law, who felt peculiarly interested in the fate of the murdered man, confirmed him in his former resolution, to let the law take its course.

The relatives of D'Horn were now reduced to the last extremity. The Prince de Robec Montmorency, despairing of other methods, found means to penetrate into the dungeon of the criminal, and offering him a cup of poison, implored him to save them from disgrace. The Count d'Horn turned away his head, and refused to take it. Montmorency pressed him once more, and losing all patience at his continued refusal, turned on his heel, and exclaiming, "Die, then, as thou wilt, mean-spirited wretch! thou art fit only to perish by the hands of the hangman!" left him to his fate.

D'Horn himself petitioned the Regent that he might be beheaded, but Law, who exercised more influence over his mind than any other person, with the exception of the notorious Abbé Dubois, his tutor, insisted that he could not in justice succumb to the self-interested views of the D'Horns. The Regent had from the first been of the same opinion, and within six days after the commission of their crime, D'Horn and Mille were broken on the wheel in the Place de Grève. The other assassin, Lestang, was never apprehended.

This prompt and severe justice was highly pleasing to the populace of Paris; even M. de Quincampoix, as they called Law, came in for a share of their approbation for having induced the Regent to show no favour to a patrician. But the number of robberies and assassinations did not diminish. No sympathy was shown for rich jobbers when they were plundered: the general laxity of public morals, conspicuous enough before, was rendered still more so by its rapid pervasion of the middle classes, who had hitherto remained comparatively pure, between the open vices of the class above and the hidden crimes of the class below them. The pernicious love of gambling diffused itself through society, and bore all public, and nearly all private, virtue before it.

For a time, while confidence lasted, an impetus was given to trade, which could not fail to be beneficial. In Paris, especially, the good results were felt. Strangers flocked into the capital from every part, bent, not only upon making money, but on spending it. The Duchess of Orleans, mother of the Regent, computes the increase of the population during this time, from the great influx of strangers from all parts of the world, at 305,000 souls. The housekeepers were obliged to make up beds in garrets, kitchens, and even stables, for the accommodation of lodgers; and the town was so full of carriages and vehicles of every description, that they were obliged in the principal streets to drive at a foot-pace for fear of accidents. The looms of the country worked with unusual activity, to supply rich laces, silks, broad-cloth, and velvets, which being paid for in abundant paper, increased in price four-fold. Provisions shared the general advance; bread, meat, and vegetables were sold at prices greater than had ever before been known; while the wages of labour rose in exactly the same proportion. The artisan, who formerly gained fifteen sous per diem, now gained sixty. New houses were built in every direction; an illusory prosperity shone over the land, and so dazzled the eyes of the whole nation that none could see the dark cloud on the horizon, announcing the storm that was too rapidly approaching.

Law himself, the magician whose wand had wrought so surprising a change, shared, of course, in the general prosperity. His wife and daughter were courted by the highest nobility, and their alliance sought by the heirs of ducal and princely houses. He bought two splendid estates in different parts of France, and entered into a negotiation with the family of the Duke de Sully for the purchase of the Marquisate of Rosny. His religion being an obstacle to his advancement, the Regent promised, if he would publicly conform to the Catholic faith, to make him comptroller-general of the finances. Law, who had no more real religion than any other professed gambler, readily agreed, and was confirmed by the Abbé de Tencin in the cathedral of Melun, in presence of a great crowd of spectators.[8] On the following day he was elected honorary churchwarden of the

8. The following squib was circulated on the occasion:-

"Foin de ton zéle séraphique,
Malheureux Abbé de Tencin,
Depuis que Law est Catholique,
Tout le royaume est Capucin!"

Thus, somewhat weakly and paraphrastically rendered by Justansond, in his translation of the "Memoirs of Louis XV":--

"Tencin, a curse on thy seraphic zeal,
Which by persuasion hath contrived the means
To make the Scotchman at our altars kneel,
Since which we all are poor as Capucines?"

parish of St. Roch, upon which occasion he made it a present of the sum of five hundred thousand livres. His charities, always magnificent, were not always so ostentatious. He gave away great sums privately, and no tale of real distress ever reached his ears in vain.

At this time, he was by far the most influential person of the state. The Duke of Orleans had so much confidence in his sagacity, and the success of his plans, that he always consulted him upon every matter of moment. He was by no means unduly elevated by his prosperity, but remained the same simple, affable, sensible man that he had shown himself in adversity. His gallantry, which was always delightful to the fair objects of it, was of a nature, so kind, so gentlemanly, and so respectful, that not even a lover could have taken offence at it. If upon any occasion he showed any symptoms of haughtiness, it was to the cringing nobles, who lavished their adulation upon him till it became fulsome. He often took pleasure in seeing how long he could make them dance attendance upon him for a single favour. To such of his own countrymen as by chance visited Paris, and sought an interview with him, he was, on the contrary, all politeness and attention. When Archibald Campbell, Earl of Islay, and afterwards Duke of Argyle, called upon him in the Place Vendôme, he had to pass through an ante-chamber crowded with persons of the first distinction, all anxious to see the great financier, and have their names put down as first on the list of some new subscription. Law himself was quietly sitting in his library, writing a letter to the gardener at his paternal estate of Lauriston about the planting of some cabbages! The Earl stayed for a considerable time, played a game of piquet with his countryman, and left him, charmed with his ease, good sense, and good breeding.

Among the nobles who, by means of the public credulity at this time, gained sums sufficient to repair their ruined fortunes, may be mentioned the names of the Dukes de Bourbon, de Guiche, de la Force,[9] de Chaulnes, and d'Antin; the Marechal d'Estrées, the Princes de Rohan, de Poix, and de León. The Duke de Bourbon, son of Louis XIV by Madame de Montespan, was peculiarly fortunate in his speculations in Mississippi paper. He rebuilt the royal residence of Chantilly in a style of unwonted magnificence, and, being passionately fond of horses, he erected a range of stables, which were long renowned throughout Europe, and imported a hundred and fifty of the finest racers from England, to improve the breed in France. He bought a large extent of country in Picardy, and became possessed of nearly all the valuable lands lying between the Oise and the Somme.

When fortunes such as these were gained, it is no wonder that Law should have been almost worshipped by the mercurial population. Never was monarch more flattered than he was. All the small poets and *littérateurs* of the day poured floods of adulation upon him. According to them he was the saviour of the country, the tutelary divinity of France; wit was in all his words, goodness in all his looks, and wisdom in all his actions. So great a crowd followed his carriage whenever he went abroad, that the Regent sent him a troop of horse as his permanent escort, to clear the streets before him.

It was remarked at this time, that Paris had never before been so full of objects of elegance and luxury. Statues, pictures, and tapestries were imported in great quantities from foreign

9. The Duke de la Force gained considerable sums, not only by jobbing in the stocks, but in dealing in porcelain, spices, &c. It was debated for a length of time in the Parliament of Paris whether he had not, in his quality of spice-merchant, forfeited his rank in the peerage. It was decided in the negative. A caricature of him was made, dressed as a street porter, carrying a large bale of spices on his back, with the inscription, "Admirez La Force."

countries, and found a ready market. All those pretty trifles in the way of furniture and ornament which the French excel in manufacturing, were no longer the exclusive play-things of the aristocracy, but were to be found in abundance in the houses of traders and the middle classes in general. Jewellery of the most costly description was brought to Paris as the most favourable mart. Among the rest, the famous diamond, bought by the Regent, and called by his name, and which long adorned the crown of France. It was purchased for the sum of two millions of livres, under circumstances which show that the Regent was not so great a gainer as some of his subjects, by the impetus which trade had received. When the diamond was first offered to him, he refused to buy it, although he desired, above all things, to possess it, alleging as his reason, that his duty to the country he governed would not allow him to spend so large a sum of the public money for a mere jewel. This valid and honourable excuse threw all the ladies of the court into alarm, and nothing was heard for some days but expressions of regret, that so rare a gem should be allowed to go out of France; no private individual being rich enough to buy it. The Regent was continually importuned about it; but all in vain, until the Duke de St. Simon, who, with all his ability, was something of a twaddler, undertook the weighty business. His entreaties, being seconded by Law, the good-natured Regent gave his consent, leaving to Law's ingenuity to find the means to pay for it. The owner took security for the payment of the sum of two millions of livres within a stated period, receiving, in the mean time, the interest of five per cent. upon that amount, and being allowed, besides, all the valuable clippings of the gem. St. Simon, in his Memoirs, relates, with no little complacency, his share in this transaction. After describing the diamond to be as large as a greengage, of a form nearly round, perfectly white, and without flaw, and weighing more than five hundred grains, he concludes with a chuckle, by telling the world, "that he takes great credit to himself for having induced the Regent to make so illustrious a purchase." In other words, he was proud that he had induced him to sacrifice his duty, and buy a bauble for himself, at an extravagant price, out of the public money.

Thus the system continued to flourish till the commencement of the year 1720. The warnings of the Parliament, that too great a creation of paper money would, sooner or later, bring the country to bankruptcy, were disregarded. The Regent, who knew nothing whatever of the philosophy of finance, thought that a system which had produced such good effects could never be carried to excess. If five hundred millions of paper had been of such advantage, five hundred millions additional would be of still greater advantage. This was the grand error of the Regent, and which Law did not attempt to dispel. The extraordinary avidity of the people kept up the delusion; and the higher the price of Indian and Mississippi stock, the more *billets de banque* were issued to keep pace with it. The edifice thus reared might not unaptly be compared to the gorgeous palace erected by Potemkin, that princely barbarian of Russia, to surprise and please his imperial mistress: huge blocks of ice were piled one upon another; ionic pillars, of chastest workmanship, in ice, formed a noble portico; and a dome, of the same material, shone in the sun, which had just strength enough to gild, but not to melt it. It glittered afar, like a palace of crystals and diamonds; but there came one warm breeze from the south, and the stately building dissolved away, till none were able even to gather up the fragments. So with Law and his paper system. No sooner did the breath of popular mistrust blow steadily upon it, than it fell to ruins, and none could raise it up again.

The first slight alarm that was occasioned was early in 1720. The Prince de Conti, offended that Law should have denied him fresh shares in India stock, at his own price, sent to his bank to demand payment in specie of so enormous a quantity of notes, that three waggons were required for its transport. Law complained to the Regent, and urged on his attention the mischief that would be done, if such an example found many imitators. The Regent was but too well aware of it, and, sending for the Prince de Conti, ordered him, under penalty of his high displeasure, to refund to the Bank two-thirds of the specie which he had withdrawn from it. The Prince was forced to obey the despotic mandate. Happily for Law's credit, De Conti was an unpopular man: everybody condemned his meanness and cupidity, and agreed that Law had been hardly treated. It is strange, however, that so narrow an escape should not have made both Law and the Regent more anxious to restrict their issues. Others were soon found who imitated, from motives of distrust, the example which had been set by De Conti in revenge. The more acute stockjobbers imagined justly that prices could not continue to rise for ever. Bourdon and La Richardière, renowned for their extensive operations in the funds, quietly and in small quantities at a time, converted their notes into specie, and sent it away to foreign countries. They also bought as much as they could conveniently carry of plate and expensive jewellery, and sent it secretly away to England or to Holland. Vermalet, a jobber, who sniffed the coming storm, procured gold and silver coin to the amount of nearly a million of livres, which he packed in a farmer's cart, and covered over with hay and cow-dung. He then disguised himself in the dirty smock-frock, or *blouse*, of a peasant, and drove his precious load in safety into Belgium. From thence he soon found means to transport it to Amsterdam.

Hitherto no difficulty had been experienced by any class in procuring specie for their wants. But this system could not long be carried on without causing a scarcity. The voice of complaint was heard on every side, and inquiries being instituted, the cause was soon discovered. The council debated long on the remedies to be taken, and Law, being called on for his advice, was of opinion, that an edict should be published, depreciating the value of coin five per cent. below that of paper. The edict was published accordingly; but, failing of its intended effect, was followed by another, in which the depreciation was increased to ten per cent. The payments of the bank were at the same time restricted to one hundred livres in gold, and ten in silver. All these measures were nugatory to restore confidence in the paper, though the restriction of cash payments within limits so extremely narrow kept up the credit of the Bank.

Notwithstanding every effort to the contrary, the precious metals continued to be conveyed to England and Holland. The little coin that was left in the country was carefully treasured, or hidden until the scarcity became so great, that the operations of trade could no longer be carried on. In this emergency, Law hazarded the bold experiment of forbidding the use of specie altogether. In February 1720 an edict was published, which, instead of restoring the credit of the paper, as was intended, destroyed it irrecoverably, and drove the country to the very brink of revolution. By this famous edict it was forbidden to any person whatever to have more than five hundred livres (20l.) of coin in his possession, under pain of a heavy fine, and confiscation of the sums found. It was also forbidden to buy up jewellery, plate, and precious stones, and informers were encouraged to make search for offenders, by the promise of one-half the amount they might discover. The whole country sent up a cry of distress at this unheard-of tyranny. The most odious persecution daily took place. The privacy of families was violated by the intrusion of informers and their agents. The most virtuous and honest were denounced for the crime of having been seen with a *louis d'or* in their possession. Servants betrayed their masters, one citizen became a spy upon his neighbour, and arrests and confiscations so multiplied, that the courts found a difficulty in getting through the immense increase of business thus occasioned. It was sufficient for an informer to say that he suspected any person of concealing money in his house, and immediately a search-warrant was granted. Lord Stair, the English ambassador, said, that it was now impossible to doubt of the sincerity of Law's conversion to the Catholic religion; he had established the inquisition, after having given abundant evidence of his faith in transubstantiation, by turning so much gold into paper.

Every epithet that popular hatred could suggest was showered upon the Regent and the unhappy Law. Coin, to any amount above five hundred livres, was an illegal tender, and nobody would take paper if he could help it. No one knew to-day what his notes would be worth to-morrow. "Never," says Duclos, in his Secret Memoirs of the Regency, "was seen a more capricious government-never was a more frantic tyranny exercised by hands less firm. It is inconceivable to those who were witnesses of the horrors of those times, and who look back upon them now as on a dream, that a sudden revolution did not break out - that Law and the Regent did not perish by a tragical death. They were both held in horror, but the people confined themselves to complaints; a sombre and timid despair, a stupid consternation, had seized upon all, and men's minds were too vile even to be capable of a courageous crime." It would appear that, at one time, a movement of the people was organised. Seditious writings were posted up against the walls, and were sent, in hand-bills, to the houses of the most conspicuous people. One of them, given in the "Mémoires de la Régence," was to the following effect:- "Sir and Madam,-This is to give you notice that a St. Bartholomew's Day will be enacted again on Saturday and Sunday, if affairs do not alter. You are desired not to stir out, nor you, nor your servants. God preserve you from the flames! Give notice to your neighbours. Dated Saturday, May 25th, 1720." The immense number of spies with which the city was infested rendered the people mistrustful of one another, and beyond some trifling disturbances made in the evening by an insignificant group, which was soon dispersed, the peace of the capital was not compromised.

The value of shares in the Louisiana, or Mississippi stock, had fallen very rapidly, and few indeed were found to believe the tales that had once been told of the immense wealth of that region. A last effort was therefore tried to restore the public confidence in the Mississippi project. For this purpose, a general conscription of all the poor wretches in Paris was made by order of government. Upwards of six thousand of the very refuse of the population were impressed, as if in time of war, and were provided with clothes and tools to be embarked for New Orleans, to work in the gold mines alleged to abound there. They were paraded day after day through the streets with their pikes and shovels, and then sent off in small detachments to the out-ports to be shipped for America. Two-thirds of them never reached their destination, but dispersed themselves over the country, sold their tools for what they could get, and returned to their old course of life. In less than three weeks afterwards, one-half of them were to be found again in Paris. The manoeuvre, however, caused a trifling advance in Mississippi stock. Many persons of superabundant gullibility believed that operations had begun in earnest in the new Golconda, and that gold and silver ingots would again be found in France.

In a constitutional monarchy some surer means would have been found for the restoration of public credit. In England, at a subsequent period, when a similar delusion had brought on similar distress, how different were the measures taken to repair the evil; but in France, unfortunately, the remedy was left to the authors of the mischief. The arbitrary will of the Regent, which endeavoured to extricate the country, only plunged it deeper into the mire. All payments were ordered to be made in paper, and between the 1st of February and the end of May, notes were fabricated to the amount of upwards of 1500 millions of livres, or 60,000,000*l*. But the alarm once sounded, no art could make the people feel the slightest confidence in paper which was not exchangeable into metal. M. Lambert, the President of the Parliament of Paris, told the Regent to his face that he would rather have a hundred thousand livres in gold or silver than five millions in the notes of his bank. When such was the general feeling, the superabundant issues of paper but increased the evil, by rendering still more enormous the disparity between the amount of specie and notes in circulation. Coin, which it was the object of the Regent to depreciate, rose in value on every fresh attempt to diminish it. In February, it was judged advisable that the Royal Bank should be incorporated with the Company of the Indies. An edict to that effect was published and registered by the Parliament. The state remained the guarantee for the notes of the bank, and no more were to be issued without an order in council. All the profits of the bank, since the time it had been taken out of Law's hands and made a national institution, were given over by the Regent to the Company of the Indies. This measure had the effect of raising for a short time the value of the Louisiana and other shares of the company, but it failed in placing public credit on any permanent basis.

A council of state was held in the beginning of May, at which Law, D'Argenson (his colleague in the administration of the finances), and all the ministers were present. It was then computed that the total amount of notes in circulation was 2600 millions of livres, while the coin in the country was not quite equal to half that amount. It was evident to the majority of the council that some plan must be adopted to equalise the currency. Some proposed that the notes should be reduced to the value of the specie, while others proposed that the nominal value of the specie should be raised till it was on an equality with the paper. Law is said to have opposed both these projects, but failing in suggesting any other, it was agreed that the notes should be depreciated one-half. On the 21st of May, an edict was accordingly issued, by which it was decreed that the shares of the Company of the Indies, and the notes of the bank, should gradually diminish in value, till at the end of a year they should only pass current for one half of their nominal worth. The Parliament refused to register the edict-the greatest outcry was excited, and the state of the country became so alarming, that, as the only means of preserving tranquillity, the council of the regency was obliged to stultify its own proceedings, by publishing within seven days another edict, restoring the notes to their original value.

On the same day (the 27th of May) the bank stopped payment in specie. Law and D'Argenson were both dismissed from the ministry. The weak, vacillating, and cowardly Regent threw the blame of all the mischief upon Law, who, upon presenting himself at the Palais Royal, was refused admitance. At nightfall, however, he was sent for, and admitted into the palace by a secret door,[10] when the Regent endeavoured to console him, and made all manner of excuses for the severity with which in public he had been compelled to treat him. So capricious was his conduct, that, two days afterwards, he took him publicly to the opera, where he sat in the royal box, alongside of the Regent, who treated him with marked consideration in face of all the people. But such was the hatred against Law that the experiment had well nigh proved fatal to him. The mob assailed his carriage with stones just as he was entering his own door; and if the coachman had not made a sudden jerk into the

10. Duclos, Mémoires Secrets de la Régence.

court-yard, and the domestics closed the gate immediately, he would, in all probability, have been dragged out and torn to pieces. On the following day, his wife and daughter were also assailed by the mob as they were returning in their carriage from the races. When the Regent was informed of these occurrences he sent Law a strong detachment of Swiss guards, who were stationed night and day in the court of his residence. The public indignation at last increased so much, that Law, finding his own house, even with this guard, insecure, took refuge in the Palais Royal, in the apartments of the Regent.

The Chancellor, D'Aguesseau, who had been dismissed in 1718 for his opposition to the projects of Law, was now recalled to aid in the restoration of credit. The Regent acknowledged too late, that he had treated with unjustifiable harshness and mistrust one of the ablest, and perhaps the sole honest public man of that corrupt period. He had retired ever since his disgrace to his country-house at Fresnes, where, in the midst of severe but delightful philosophic studies, he had forgotten the intrigues of an unworthy court. Law himself, and the Chevalier de Conflans, a gentleman of the Regent's household, were despatched in a post-chaise, with orders to bring the ex-chancellor to Paris along with them. D'Aguesseau consented to render what assistance he could, contrary to the advice of his friends, who did not approve that he should accept any recall to office of which Law was the bearer. On his arrival in Paris, five counsellors of the Parliament were admitted to confer with the Commissary of Finance, and on the 1st of June an order was published, abolishing the law which made it criminal to amass coin to the amount of more than five hundred livres. Every one was permitted to have as much specie as he pleased. In order that the bank-notes might be withdrawn, twenty-five millions of new notes were created, on the security of the revenues of the city of Paris, at two-and-a-half per cent. The bank-notes withdrawn were publicly burned in front of the Hôtel de Ville. The new notes were principally of the value of ten livres each; and on the 10th of June the bank was re-opened, with a sufficiency of silver coin to give in change for them.

These measures were productive of considerable advantage. All the population of Paris hastened to the bank, to get coin for their small notes; and silver becoming scarce, they were paid in copper. Very few complained that this was too heavy, although poor fellows might be continually seen toiling and sweating along the streets, laden with more than they could comfortably carry, in the shape of change for fifty livres. The crowds around the bank were so great, that hardly a day passed that some one was not pressed to death. On the 9th of July, the multitude was so dense and clamorous that the guards stationed at the entrance of the Mazarin Gardens closed the gate, and refused to admit any more. The crowd became incensed, and flung stones through the railings upon the soldiers. The latter, incensed in their turn, threatened to fire upon the people. At that instant one of them was hit by a stone, and, taking up his piece, he fired into the crowd. One man fell dead immediately, and another was severely wounded. It was every instant expected that a general attack would have been commenced upon the bank; but the gates of the Mazarin Gardens being opened to the crowd, who saw a whole troop of soldiers, with their bayonets fixed, ready to receive them, they contented themselves by giving vent to their indignation in groans and hisses.

Eight days afterwards the concourse of people was so tremendous, that fifteen persons were squeezed to death at the doors of the bank. The people were so indignant that they took three of the bodies on stretchers before them, and proceeded, to the number of seven or eight thousand, to the gardens of the Palais Royal, that they might show the Regent the misfortunes that he and Law had brought upon the country. Law's coachman, who was sitting on the box of his master's carriage, in the court-yard of the palace, happened to have more zeal than discretion, and, not liking that the mob should abuse his master, he said, loud enough to be overheard by several persons, that they were all blackguards, and deserved to be hanged. The mob immediately set upon him, and, thinking that Law was in the carriage, broke it to pieces. The imprudent coachman narrowly escaped with his life. No further mischief was done; a body of troops making their appearance, the crowd quietly dispersed, after an assurance had been given by the Regent that the three bodies they had brought to show him should be decently buried at his own expense. The Parliament was sitting at the time of this uproar, and the President took upon himself to go out and see what was the matter. On his return he informed the councillors, that Law's carriage had been broken by the mob. All the members rose simultaneously, and expressed their joy by a loud shout, while one man, more zealous in his hatred than the rest, exclaimed, "*And Law himself, is he torn to pieces*?"[11]

Much undoubtedly depended on the credit of the Company of the Indies, which was answerable for so great a sum to the nation. It was, therefore, suggested in the council of the ministry, that any privileges which could be granted to enable it to fulfil its engagements, would be productive of the best results. With this end in view, it was proposed that the exclusive privilege of all maritime commerce should be secured to it, and an edict to

11. The Duchess of Orleans gives a different version of this story; but whichever be the true one, the manifestation of such feeling in a legislative assembly was not very creditable. She says, that the President was so transported with joy, that he was seized with a rhyming fit, and, returning into the hall, exclaimed to the members:-

"Messieurs ! Messieurs ! bonne nouvelle!
Le carfosse de Lass est reduit en canelle!"

that effect was published. But it was unfortunately forgotten that by such a measure all the merchants of the country would be ruined. The idea of such an immense privilege was generally scouted by the nation, and petition on petition was presented to the Parliament, that they would refuse to register the decree. They refused accordingly, and the Regent, remarking that they did nothing but fan the flame of sedition, exiled them to Blois. At the intercession of D'Aguesseau, the place of banishment was changed to Pontoise, and thither accordingly the councillors repaired, determined to set the Regent at defiance. They made every arrangement for rendering their temporary exile as agreeable as possible. The President gave the most elegant suppers, to which he invited all the gayest and wittiest company of Paris. Every night there was a concert and ball for the ladies. The usually grave and solemn judges and councillors joined in cards and other diversions, leading for several weeks a life of the most extravagant pleasure, for no other purpose than to show the Regent of how little consequence they deemed their banishment, and that when they will edit, they could make Pontoise a pleasanter residence than Paris.

Of all the nations in the world the French are the most renowned for singing over their grievances. Of that country it has been remarked with some truth, that its whole history may be traced in its songs. When Law, by the utter failure of his best-laid plans, rendered himself obnoxious, satire of course seized hold upon him, and, while caricatures of his person appeared in all the shops, the streets resounded with songs, in which neither he nor the Regent was spared. Many of these songs were far from decent; and one of them in particular counselled the application of all his notes to the most ignoble use to which paper can be applied. But the following, preserved in the letters of the Duchess of Orleans, was the best and the most popular, and was to be heard for months in all the carrefours of Paris.

The application of the chorus is happy enough:-

Aussitôt que Lass arriva
Dans notre bonne ville,
Monsieur le Régent publia
Que Lass serait utile
Pour rétablir la nation.
La faridondaine! la faridondon!
Mais il nous a tous enrichi,
Biribi!
A la façon de Barbari,
Mon ami!

Ce parpaillot, pour attirer
Tout l'argent de la France,
Songea d'abord à s'assurer
De notre confiance.
Il fit son abjuration,
La faridondaine! la faridondon!
Mais le fourbe s'est converti,
Biribi!
A la façon de Barbari,
Mon ami!

Lass, le fils ainé de Satan
Nous met tous à l'aumône,
Il nous a pris tout notre argent

Et n'en rend à personne.

Mais le Ré gent, humain et bon,

La faridondaine! la faridondon!

Nous rendra ce qu'on nous a pris,

Biribi!

A la façon de Barbari,

Mon ami!

The following smart epigram is of the same date:-

Lundi, j'achetai des actions;

Mardi, je gagnai des millions;

Mercredi, j'arrangeai mon ménage,

Jeudi, je pris un équipage,

Vendredi, je m'en fus au bal,

Et Samedi, a l'Hôpital.

Among the caricatures that were abundantly published, and that showed as plainly as graver matters, that the nation had awakened to a sense of its folly, was one, a facsimile of which is preserved in the " Mémoires de la Régence." It was thus described by its author: "The 'Goddess of Shares,' in her triumphal car, driven by the Goddess of Folly. Those who are drawing the car are impersonations of the Mississippi, with his wooden leg, the South Sea, the Bank of England, the Company of the West of Senegal, and of various assurances. Lest the car should not roll fast enough, the agents of these companies, known by their long fox-tails and their cunning looks, turn round the spokes of the wheels, upon which are marked the names of the several stocks, and their value, sometimes high and sometimes low, according to the turns of the wheel. Upon the ground are the merchandise, day-books and ledgers of legitimate commerce, crushed under the chariot of Folly. Behind is an immense crowd of persons, of all ages, sexes, and conditions, clamoring after Fortune, and fighting with each other to get a portion of the shares which she distributes so bountifully among them. In the clouds sits a demon, blowing bubbles of soap, which are also the objects of the admiration and cupidity of the crowd, who jump upon one another's backs to reach them ere they burst. Right in the pathway of the car, and blocking up the passage, stands a large building, with three doors, through one of which it must pass, if it proceeds further, and all the crowd along with it. Over the first door are the words, "*Hôpital des Foux*," over the second, "*Hôpital des Malades*," and over the third, "*Hôpital des Gueux*." Another caricature represented Law sitting in a large cauldron, boiling over the flames of popular madness, surrounded by an impetuous multitude, who were pouring all their gold and silver into it, and receiving gladly in exchange the bits of paper which he distributed among them by hands full.

While this excitement lasted, Law took good care not to expose himself unguarded in the streets. Shut up in the apartments of the Regent, he was secure from all attack, and, whenever he ventured abroad, it was either *incognito*, or in one of the Royal carriages, with a powerful escort. An amusing anecdote is recorded of the detestation in which he was held by the people, and the ill treatment he would have met, had he fallen into their hands. A gentleman, of the name of Boursel, was passing in his carriage down the Rue St. Antoine, when his further progress was stayed by a hackney-coach that had blocked up the road. M. Boursel's servant called impatiently to the hackney-coachman to get out of the way, and, on his refusal, struck him a blow on the face. A crowd was soon drawn together by the disturbance, and M. Boursel got out of the carriage to restore order. The hackney-coachman, imagining that he had now another assailant, bethought him of an expedient to rid himself of both, and called out as loudly as he was able, "Help! help! murder! murder! Here are Law and his servant going to kill me! Help! help!" At this cry, the people came out of their shops, armed with sticks and other weapons, while the mob gathered stones to inflict summary vengeance upon the supposed financier. Happily for M. Boursel and his servant, the door of the church of the Jesuits stood wide open, and, seeing the fearful odds against them, they rushed towards it with all speed. They reached the altar, pursued by the people, and would have been ill treated even there, if, finding the door open leading to the sacristy, they had not sprang through, and closed it after them. The mob were then persuaded to leave the church by the alarmed and indignant priests; and, finding M. Boursel's carriage still in the streets, they vented their ill-will against it, and did it considerable damage.

The twenty-five millions secured on the municipal revenues of the city of Paris, bearing so low an interest as two and a half per cent., were not very popular among the large holders of Mississippi stock. The conversion of the securities was, therefore, a work of considerable difficulty; for many preferred to retain the falling paper of Law's Company, in the hope that a favourable turn might take place. On the 15th of August, with a view to hasten the conversion, an edict was passed, declaring that all notes for sums between one thousand and ten thousand livres; should not pass current, except for the purchase of annuities and bank accounts, or for the payment of instalments still due on the shares of the company.

In October following another edict was passed, depriving these notes of all value whatever after the month of November next ensuing. The management of the mint, the farming of the revenue, and all the other advantages and privileges of the India, or Mississippi Company, were taken from them, and they were reduced to a mere private company. This was the deathblow to the whole system, which had now got into the hands of its enemies. Law had lost all influence in the Council of Finance, and the company, being despoiled of its immunities, could no longer hold out the shadow of a prospect of being able to fulfil its engagements. All those suspected of illegal profits at the time the public delusion was at its height, were sought out and amerced in heavy fines. It was previously ordered that a list of the original proprietors should be made out, and that such persons as still retained their shares should place them in deposit with the company, and that those who had neglected to complete the shares for which they had put down their names, should now purchase them of the company, at the rate of 13,500 livres for each share of 500 livres. Rather than submit to pay this enormous sum for stock which was actually at a discount, the shareholders packed up all their portable effects, and endeavoured to find a refuge in foreign countries. Orders were immediately issued to the authorities at the ports and frontiers, to apprehend all travellers who sought to leave the kingdom, and keep them in custody, until it was ascertained whether they had any plate or jewellery with them, or were concerned in the late stock-jobbing. Against such few as escaped, the punishment of death was recorded, while the most arbitrary proceedings were instituted against those who remained.

Law himself, in a moment of despair, determined to leave a country where his life was no longer secure. He at first only demanded permission to retire from Paris to one of his country seats; a permission which the Regent cheerfully granted. The latter was much affected at the unhappy turn affairs had taken, but his faith continued unmoved in the truth and efficacy of Law's financial system. His eyes were opened to his own errors, and during the few remaining years of his life, he constantly longed for an opportunity of again establishing the system upon a securer basis. At Law's last interview with the Prince, he is reported to have said-"I confess that I have committed many faults; I committed them because I am a man, and all men are liable to error; but I declare to you most solemnly that none of them proceeded from wicked or dishonest motives, and that nothing of the kind will be found in the whole course of my conduct."

Two or three days after his departure the Regent sent him a very kind letter, permitting him to leave the kingdom whenever he pleased, and stating that he had ordered his passports to be made ready. He at the same time offered him any sum of money he might require. Law respectfully declined the money, and set out for Brussels in a postchaise belonging to Madame de Prie, the mistress of the Duke of Bourbon, escorted by six horse-guards. From thence he proceeded to Venice, where he remained for some months, the object of the greatest curiosity to the people, who believed him to be the possessor of enormous wealth. No opinion, however, could be more erroneous. With more generosity than could have been expected from a man who during the greatest part of his life had been a professed gambler, he had refused to enrich himself at the expense of a ruined nation. During the height of the popular frenzy for Mississippi stock, he had never doubted of the final success of his projects, in making France the richest and most powerful nation of Europe. He invested all his gains in the purchase of landed property in France - a sure proof of his own belief in the stability of his schemes. He had hoarded no plate or jewellery, and sent no money, like the dishonest jobbers, to foreign countries. His all, with the exception of one diamond, worth about five or six thousand pounds sterling, was invested in the French soil; and when he left that country, he left it almost a beggar. This fact alone ought to rescue his memory from the charge of knavery, so often and so unjustly brought against him.

As soon as his departure was known, all his estates and his valuable library were confiscated. Among the rest, an annuity of 200,000 livres, (8000*l.* sterling,) on the lives of his wife and children, which had been purchased for five millions of livres, was forfeited, notwithstanding that a special edict, drawn up for the purpose in the days of his prosperity, had expressly declared that it should never be confiscated for any cause whatever. Great discontent existed among the people that Law had been suffered to escape. The mob and the Parliament would have been pleased to have seen him hanged. The few who had not suffered by the commercial revolution, rejoiced that the *quack* had left the country; but all those (and they were by far the most numerous class) whose fortunes were implicated, regretted that his intimate knowledge of the distress of the country, and of the causes that had led to it, had not been rendered more available in discovering a remedy.

At a meeting of the Council of Finance, and the general council of the Regency, documents were laid upon the table, from which it appeared that the amount of notes in circulation was 2700 millions. The Regent was called upon to explain how it happened that there was a discrepancy between the dates at which these issues were made, and those of the edicts by which they were authorised. He might have safely taken the whole blame upon himself, but he preferred that an absent man should bear a share of it, and he therefore stated that Law, upon his own authority, had issued 1200 millions of notes at different times, and that he (the Regent) seeing that the thing had been irrevocably done, had screened Law, by antedating the decrees of the council, which authorised the augmentation. It would have been more to his credit if he had told the whole truth while he was about it, and acknowledged that it was mainly through his extravagance and impatience that Law had been induced to overstep the bounds of safe speculation. It was also ascertained that the national debt, on the1st of January, 1721, amounted to upwards of $100 millions of livres, or more than 124,000,000*l.* sterling, the interest upon which was 3,196,000*l.* A commission, or visa, was forthwith appointed to examine into all the securities of the state creditors, who were to be divided into five classes, the first four comprising those who had purchased their securities with real effects, and the latter comprising those who could give no proofs that the transactions they had entered into were real and *bona fide*. The securities of the latter were ordered to be destroyed, while those of the first four classes were subjected to a most rigid and jealous scrutiny. The result of the labours of the *visa* was a report, in which they counselled the reduction of the interest upon these securities to fifty-six millions of livres. They justified this advice by a statement of the various acts of peculation and extortion which they had discovered, and an edict to that effect was accordingly published and duly registered by the parliaments of the kingdom.

Another tribunal was afterwards established, under the title of the *Chambre de l'Arsenal*, which took cognizance of all the malversations committed in the financial departments of the government during the late unhappy period. A Master of Requests, named Falhonet, together with the Abbé Clement, and two clerks in their employ, had been concerned in divers acts of peculation, to the amount of upwards of a million of livres. The first two were sentenced to be beheaded, and the latter to be hanged; but their punishment was afterwards commuted into imprisonment for life in the Bastile. Numerous other acts of dishonesty were discovered, and punished by fine and imprisonment.

D'Argenson shared with Law and the Regent the unpopularity which had alighted upon all those concerned in the Mississippi madness. He was dismissed from his post of Chancellor, to make room for D'Aguesseau; but he retained the title of Keeper of the Seals, and was allowed to attend the councils whenever he pleased. He thought it better, however, to withdraw from Paris, and live for a time a life of seclusion at his country-seat. But he was not formed for retirement, and becoming moody and discontented, he aggravated a disease under which he had long laboured, and died in less than a twelvemonth. The populace of Paris so detested him, that they carried their hatred even to his grave. As his funeral procession passed to the church of St. Nicholas du Chardonneret, the burying-place of his family, it was beset by a riotous mob, and his two sons, who were following as chief-mourners, were obliged to drive as fast as they were able down a by-street to escape personal violence.

As regards Law, he for some time entertained a hope that he should be recalled to France, to aid in establishing its credit upon a firmer basis. The death of the Regent, in 1723, who expired suddenly, as he was sitting by the fireside conversing with his mistress, the Duchess de Phalaris, deprived him of that hope, and he was reduced to lead his former life of gambling. He was more than once obliged to pawn his diamond, the sole remnant of his vast wealth, but successful play generally enabled him to redeem it. Being persecuted by his creditors at Rome, he proceeded to Copenhagen, where he received permission from the English ministry to reside in his native country, his pardon for the murder of Mr. Wilson having been sent over to him in 1719. He was brought over in the admiral's ship, a circumstance which gave occasion for a short debate in the House of Lords. Earl Coningsby complained that a man, who had renounced both his country and his religion, should have been treated with such honour, and expressed his belief that his presence in England, at a time when the people were so bewildered by the nefarious practices of the South Sea directors, would be attended with no little danger. He gave notice of a motion on the subject; but it was allowed to drop, no other member of the House having the slightest participation in his lordship's fears. Law remained for about four years in England, and then proceeded to Venice, where he died in 1729, in very embarrassed circumstances. The following epitaph was written at the time:-

"Ci gît cet Ecossais célèbre,

Ce calculateur sans égat,

Qui, par les regles de l'algèbre,

A mis la France a l'Hôpitat."

His brother, William Law, who had been concerned with him in the administration both of the Bank and the Louisiana Company, was imprisoned in the Bastile for alleged malversation, but no guilt was ever proved against him. He was liberated after fifteen months, and became the founder of a family, which is still known in France under the title of Marquises of Lauriston.

ADAM SMITH

ON THE NATURE, ACCUMULATION AND EMPLOYMENT OF STOCK

an excerpt from

An Inquiy into the Nature and Causes of the Wealth of Nations, Book II

(1776)

ADAM SMITH

ON THE NATURE, ACCUMULATION AND EMPLOYMENT OF STOCK

ON THE NATURE, ACCUMULATION, AND EMPLOYMENT OF STOCK

That the industry of Scotland languished for want of money to employ it was the opinion of the famous Mr. Law. By establishing a bank of a particular kind, which he seems to have imagined might issue paper to the amount of the whole value of all the lands in the country, he proposed to remedy this want of money. The Parliament of Scotland, when he first proposed his project, did not think proper to adopt it. It was afterwards adopted, with some variations, by the Duke of Orleans, at that time Regent of France. The idea of the possibility of multiplying paper to almost any extent was the real foundation of what is called the Mississippi scheme, the most extravagant project both of banking and stock-jobbing that, perhaps, the world ever saw. The different operations of this scheme are explained so fully, so clearly, and with so much order and distinctness, by Mr. du Verney, in his Examination of the Political Reflections upon Commerce and Finances of Mr. du Tot, that I shall not give any account of them. The principles upon which it was founded are explained by Mr. Law himself, in a discourse concerning money and trade, which he published in Scotland when he first proposed his project. The splendid but visionary ideas which are set forth in that and some other works upon the same principles still continue to make an impression upon many people, and have, perhaps, in part, contributed to that excess of banking which has of late been complained of both in Scotland and in other places.

ADAM SMITH

OF THE SCHEME OF MR. LAW

from

Lectures on Jurispridence

(1763)

ADAM SMITH

OF THE SCHEME OF MR. LAW

OF THE SCHEME OF MR. LAW

The last bad effect that shall be taken notice of is the notion of Mr. Law, a Scotch merchant. He thought that national opulence consists in money, and that the value of gold and silver is arbitrary, and depends on constitution and agreement. He imagined that the idea of value might be brought to paper, and it preferred to money. If this could be done, he thought it would be a great convenience, as the government then might do what it pleased, raise armies, pay soldiers, and be at any expense whatever. Mr. Law proposed his scheme to the Scotch parliament in 1701.[1] It was rejected, and he went over to France, where his project was relished by the Duke of Orleans. In this book [2] he agrees with the fore-mentioned writers that, the balance of trade being against a nation, it must soon be

---

1. A mistake for '1705.' In the 2nd edition of *Money and Trade*, 1720, the bookseller requests the reader to receive favourably 'the following pages, which consist of some heads of a scheme which Mr. Law proposed to the Parliament of Scotland in the year 1705.' The year given in the text above was the date of Law's *Proposals and Reasons for Constituting a Council of Trade in Scotland.*

2. i.e. *Money and Trade Considered, with a Proposal for Supplying the Nation with Money*, 1705.

drained of its money. In order to turn the balance of trade in our favours, he proposed to the Scotch Parliament the following scheme:

As there was little gold or silver in this country he thought they might fall upon some other method of creating money, independent of it, to wit, by paper. On this account he proposed the erecting of a land bank at Edinburgh, in which it is to be observed, he falls into many blunders concerning tenures and the nature of property. At this bank they were to keep by them only twenty or thirty thousand pounds to answer small demands, and to give out notes for land. For two acres of arable land they were to issue out a note of equal value, and if any extraordinary demand was made upon them, they would pay so much of it in money, and so much in land. By this means in a very short time the whole land of Scotland would go from hand to hand, as a twenty-shilling note does.[3]

As this project never was executed, it is hard to say what the consequence might have been; it is, however, obviously liable to the following inconveniences. Taking the land rent of Scotland at five millions per annum, though it be much more, at twenty years' purchase it amounts to an hundred millions; there would then be just so much currency in the country and if one million was then necessary for circulation there would just be ninety-nine millions for no purpose, as none of it could go abroad; they would not have been able to maintain one man more than formerly, as their food, clothes, and lodging would not have been increased, and every commodity would have risen to ninety-nine times its present value.

Mr. Law, not meeting with the encouragement he expected, went over to France in the year [4] 1714, and, as was before

3. This paragraph appears to be intended as a summary of ch. vii. of *Money and Trade.Considered.*

4. MS. reads 'years.'

mentioned, found favour with the Duke of Orleans, then[5] Regent, and got liberty to erect a bank here, which at first was only to the extent of six millions of livres [6] or £320,0[00] sterling. From this beginning he carried it on to a very great height, issued out many notes, and in a short time engrossed the whole circulation of France. As Mr. Law's notes were received in payment of the revenue,[7] this contributed to the success of the scheme. This, too, had a greater effect in France than it could have had here, considering the number of taxes, and the manner in which they are levied. By this and other circumstances, his notes were always at par with gold and silver, especially as they were making continual changes in their coin. About that time [8] twenty-eight livres, which were equal to eight ounces of pure silver, were raised to sixty, and as a diminution of coin is always the consequent of a sudden rise,[9] this was daily expected. Mr. Law made his notes payable in what was called the money of the day.[10] Instead of promising to pay his notes, as we would say, in pounds sterling, he did it in crowns and half-crowns, which was a very proper method to make them par with

5. 'Then' refers not to 1714, but to the time when Law found sufficient favour to get liberty to erect a bank. Louis XIV died on Sept. 1, 1715. Orleans had seen Law, and spoken of him as 'un homme de qui il pourrait tirer des lumières' before that date (Saint-Simon, *Mémoires*, ed. Chéruel et Regnier, tom. xiii. p. 49).

6. Paris Duverney, *Examen du livre intitulé Réflexions politiques sur les finances et le commerce,* 1740, tom. i. p. 207.

7. Ibid. p. 210.

8. 'About that time' apparently stands for 'between 1715 and May, 1718.' Dutot, *Réflexions politiques sur les finances et le commerce*, 1738, in Daire's *Économistes financiers*, pp. 810, 847; and Duverney, *Examen*, tom. i. pp. 216, 217.

9. Above, p. 189.

10. 'En écus du poids et titre du jour.' Duverney, *Examen*, tom. i. p. 209

gold and silver. Suppose that our coin were raised to double, a half-crown would become a crown, and so in this manner the bank notes and money would rise and fall together.[11]

As Law wanted to make his notes above par, he fell upon the following scheme. He issued out his bank notes payable in livres tournois, by which, when the coin came to be diminished, he would not be obliged to pay above one-half[12]. The coin was not received in the market or elsewhere, as the diminution was still expected, and did not come for some time. This favoured his design, and kept the notes above par, by which the credit of his bank was established.

The next step Mr. Law fell upon was the relieving of the

---

11. It must be remembered that in Adam Smith's time the pound sterling was just as much a mere money of account as the French livre. Its practical identification with a particular coin is of later date, and even now that coin is not called a pound, but a sovereign. Raising our coin to double would mean halving the quantity of silver coined into twenty shillings or '£1.' Law's notes for écus of a certain weight and fineness resembled Drummond's notes for guineas mentioned in W. of N. bk. i. ch. v. vol. i. p. 42.

12. There appears to be some mistake or omission here. A diminution of the coin, i. e. a reduction of the number of livres in an ecu of a certain weight and fineness would obviously increase the bullion value of notes for livres. So, if the coin were diminished 50 per cent, and no change made as regards the notes, Law would be obliged to pay double, not half. It may, however, have been supposed that the notes would be arbitrarily reduced when the coin was diminished, as an edict was soon issued declaring that this would not under any circumstances take place. The next two sentences in the text above describe the natural effect of this edict (see Duverney, *Examen*, tom. i. pp.235, 236), and do not at all follow from the statement that Law would not be obliged to pay above a half.

public debts, which amounted to 200[0] millions.[13] As he saw the diminution must needs come, he took another method to keep up his notes. He got a grant of the exclusive privilege of trading to Canada, and established the Mississippi Company. To this he joined the African, the Turkey, and the East India companies. He also farmed the tobacco and all the public revenues of France at 52 millions,[14] for in France the whole revenue is farmed by one man, who undertakes it and levies it without excisemen, and the farmers there are the richest in the country, and must be skilled in the finances and public revenues.[15] Mr. Law undertook this, and, having the whole trade of the country monopolized, it was difficult to say what profits he would make. He wanted to lend the government 80 or 90 millions [sterling], which he could easily do by issuing notes to that value, but then he saw that they would soon return upon him. To prevent this, his invention was set on work, and we shall see how far he succeeded. As the company he erected seemed to be in a very flourishing condition, shares were purchased in it at a very considerable rate. He opened a subscription to it at 500 livres, so that a navy ticket or *billet d'état* purchased a share into it, which raised them to a par, as they had for a long time been far below it. The government of France was never in such a miserable condition as then. The interest of the money which should have paid the billets d'état was seized upon for other purposes. Never was monarch more degraded than Lewis XIV. After the treaty of Utrecht he had occasion to borrow 8 millions of livres from Holland, and not only to give them his bond for 32 millions, but to get some

13. Dutot, in Daire's *Économistes financiers*, p. 806, gives the amount as 'deux milliards soixante-deux millions cent trente-huit mille une livres.'

14. Duverney, *Examen*, tom. i. p. 249. MS. reads 12 millions.

15. Duverney, *Examen*, tom. i. p. 252.

merchants to be security for him.[16] Since that was the case, we need not be surprised that the billets d'état sold at great discount, as they bore no interest, and it was quite uncertain when they would be paid. Law published a declaration that one of these, which was granted for 500 livres, should purchase a share in the company, and thus they came again to par. The people still continuing in great expectations of profit, he in a few days opened a new subscription at 5000 livres, and afterwards another at 10,000. At this time he was enabled to lend the government 1600 millions of livres at 3 per cent.[17]

Had he stopped here, it is probable that he would have answered all engagements, but his future proceedings ruined all. It was impossible that the value of shares could long continue at such a high rate. He thought, however, that it was necessary to do all that he could to keep them up, as the whole fortunes of many people were in the bank. He had issued out notes to double the circulation of the country, which raised the price of everything to an enormous pitch, and consequently the exchange was against France in all foreign trade. This was principally occasioned by his opening an office to purchase 500 livres shares at 9000 livres,[18] which obliged him to issue out many notes. People of prudence who were concerned opposed this scheme, and indeed it was the first thing that made his bank lose credit, and occasioned its dissolution. As he was not obliged to pay the capital sums, only the annual dividend of 200 livres arising from the profits,[19] he might have let them

16. Dutot, in Daire's *Économistes financiers*, p. 805, mentions these terms, and says that the loan was obtained from foreigners on the credit of a private person and his friends, but does not specify Holland.

17. Duverney, *Examen*, tom. i. pp. 250, 273, 289.

18. *Ibid.* pp. 280, 281.

19. The original fixed interest share was only 4 per cent., or 20 livres on the shares of 500 livres; but a general meeting of the company held on

fall to their original 500 without any great loss but that of reputation; but his buying up the shares occasioned his issuing out so many notes that they must of necessity return upon him. This was so much the case that he was obliged to open offices in different parts of Paris for the payment of them. When in this manner oppressed, he was making continual changes on the coin, in order to dissuade people from returning on the bank, and disgust them at gold and silver.[20] He cried up gold, but as coin cannot be kept much above the level of the metal, when it was so much depreciated, it was not taken. If a person had 20,000 guineas, as he was afraid that the coin would not continue at that value, he went to the bank and got it exchanged for notes. The same consideration prevented them from returning upon the bank, as they would there be paid in coin. By this means he not only prevented his notes from coming upon him, but filled his coffers with almost all the gold in the country. In order to accomplish this part of his scheme more perfectly, he most arbitrarily published an edict prohibiting any persons from keeping by them gold or silver, beyond a certain sum.[21] He also took away the severe penalties that were in force against the exportation of coin, and every person was allowed to export money free from duty.[22] By this means much of it went to Holland. He reasoned with himself, some instrument of change is necessary, paper, gold, and silver, at present are the medium; if gold and silver be utterly exported, paper only remains, and may be rendered the sole instrument of commerce. This he thought he had done effectually when by an edict he had swept a part into his coffers, and cleared the

Dec. 30, 1719, resolved that the dividend should be 40 per cent., or 200 livres per share, *Ibid.* pp. 215, 267, 268, 317.

20. 'Pour dégoûté les peuples des monnaies d'or et d'argent.. *Ibid.* p. 316.

21. Viz . 500 livres. Duverney, *Examen*, tom. i. p. 335.

22. *Ibid.* pp. 320, 321.

country of the remainder. They would therefore be obliged to take paper. At last, however, after a great number of expedients, he found it was impracticable. By paying out great sums, he kept off ruin for some months, but at last published an edict that all bank notes were to be paid only in one half: and indeed if he had stood to this, as some imagined he might have done, it would have been far better than to have suffered the after consequences. Upon this edict the credit of the bank was entirely broken, and the bank notes all on a sudden sunk to nothing.[23] This ruined an immense number of people. Britain can never be much hurt by the breaking of a bank, because few people keep notes by them to any value.[24] A man worth £40,000 will scarce ever have £500 of notes by him. But the breaking of this bank in France occasioned the most dreadful confusion. The greatest part of people had their whole fortunes in notes, and were reduced to a state of beggary. The only people who were safe were the stock-jobbers who had sold out in time, or with their bank notes had purchased all the valuable goods and a great deal of land, though at the highest prices. These made immense fortunes by it.

The South Sea scheme in our own country was nothing to this. Nobody was under any obligations of going into it, the government had no share in it, and the loss was but a trifle in comparison. The clamour which Law's last edict made caused it soon to be rescinded,[25] and the notes were again declared to be paid at value, but the bank never recovered its credit, and this had no effect. However, by raising the coin and other expedients, he kept it from May to October, and then [26] was obliged to leave France, which with difficulty he accomplished;

23. *Ibid.* tom.ii. pp. 6-8.

24. Above, p. 195.

25. Duverney, *Examen*, tom. Ii. P. 11.

26. In December, 1720. *Ibid.* p. 132.

his goods were confiscated and he died soon after.[27] This amazing scheme was founded on these two principles, that public opulence consists in money, and that the value of money is arbitrary, founded upon the common consent of mankind. Consistent with these principles he thought he might easily increase the public opulence if he could annex the idea of money to paper, and the government could never be at any loss to produce any effect that money could do. This scheme of Mr. Law's was by no means contemptible; he really believed in it, and was the dupe of it himself. It was thought he had provided well for himself, but it was found to be otherwise. If the Duke of Orleans had lived only a few days longer it was agreed upon that he was to have been re-established. After his death it was not thought expedient to have it put in execution.

This scheme of Law's was imitated all over Europe. It gave occasion to the South Sea Company in England, which turned out at last a mere fraud, and, could it have been carried to as great an extent as Law's, would have been productive of the same consequences. It was erected in the latter end of Queen Anne's reign, and the intention of it was to carry on a trade to the South Seas. For this purpose they bought up the greater part of the debts of the nation. Their stock, however, was not great, and the profits which could be expected from it were very inconsiderable; the expectations of the people were never greatly raised, and its fall was not very prejudicial to the nation.

27. Not till 1729.

VOLTAIRE

LAW'S SYSTEM

from

The Works of M. de Voltaire

(1761)

VOLTAIRE

LAW'S SYSTEM

LAW'S SYSTEM

All the courts of Europe were astonished to see, sometime after, in 1724 and 1725, Philip V. and Charles VI. formerly irreconcileable enemies, now united in bonds of the strictest friendship; and affairs diviated from their natural course to such a degree, that the ministry of Madrid governed the court of Vienna during a whole year. That court, whose intention had constantly been to exclude the French branch which reigned over Spain, from all access to Italy, so far lost sight of its first views as to admit a son of Philip V. and Elizabeth of Parma, his second wife, into that very country from which they formerly intended to exclude every Frenchman and every Spaniard. The emperor bestowed upon this younger son of his competitor the investiture of Parma and Placentia, and the grand dutchy of Tuscany. Though the succession of these states was not made public, Don Carlos was introduced with six thousand Spaniards; and it cost Spain only twenty thousand pistoles, which were paid at Vienna.

This imprudent step of the emperor's council was by no means one of those which are productive of happy consequences; it cost him very dear in the sequel. Every circumstance in this treaty was singular; two adverse houses united without trusting each other; the English, who had exerted their utmost efforts to dethrone Philip V. and had deprived him of Minorca and Gibraltar, were mediators in the treaty: it was signed by a Dutchman, named Ripperda, who had been raised to the dignity of duke, and was at that time very powerful in Spain; he was disgraced after having signed it, and retired to end his life in the kingdom of Morocco, where he endeavoured to establish a new religion.

In France, during this time, the regency of the duke of Orleans, which threatened to be the most tumultuous ever known, on account of the secret practices of his enemies, and the general confusion of the finances, had been the most peaceable and the most happy imaginable. The habit of obedience, to which the French had been accustomed under Lewis XIV. was the security of the regent, and of public tranquillity. The conspiracy, which had been directed under-hand by cardinal [1]

1. Alberoni, by means of the prince of Cellamare, the Spanish ambassador at Paris, intrigued with the malcontents of France; and a scheme was formed for seizing the regent, and securing the person of the young king. The duke of Orleans received the first intimation of this plot from the king of Great Britain; but the particulars were discovered by accident. The prince de Cellamare intrusted his dispatches to the abbé Portocarero, and to a son of the marquis de Montelione, who set out from Paris together in a post-chaise, and were overturned. The postilion, having on this occasion, heard the abbé declare that he would not have lost his portmanteau for an hundred thousand pistoles, informed the government of this circumstance at his return to Paris. The Spaniards were immediately pursued, overtaken and seized at Poitiers, with the portmanteau, in which were found two letters, which made the regent acquainted with the particulars of the conspiracy. The prince de Cellamare was forthwith conducted to the frontiers. The duke of Mayne, the marquis de Pompadour, and the cardinal de Polignac, with many other persons of distinction, were committed to different prisons. The regent declared war against Spain; and an army of thirty-six thousand

Alberoni, and ill managed in France, was defeated as soon as formed. The parliament, which during the minority of Lewis XIV. had commenced a civil war, on account of twelve places of master of the requests, and which had superseded the wills of Lewis XIII. and Lewis XIV. with less ceremony than if they had been the wills of private persons, scarcely had liberty to remonstrate, when the numerary value of the coin was raised to above three times its ordinary standard. His marching on foot from the great chamber to the Louvre, only drew upon him the raillery of the people. The most unjust edict that ever was published, the edict whereby all the inhabitants of the kingdom were forbid to keep by them any more than five hundred livres in ready money, did not occasion the least disturbance. The general scarcity of specie in the land; a whole people pressing in crowds to ask at an office a little money to supply their immediate occasions; paper credit, with which France was quite overwhelmed; many citizens trod to death in the crowd, and their dead bodies carried to the royal palace; I say, all this put together did not give rise to the slightest insurrection. In a word, the celebrated system of Law, which seemed calculated to ruin both the regency and the state, contributed to the support of both, by consequences which no body could foresee.

The avarice which it occasioned amongst men of all conditions, from the lowest of the vulgar to the magistrates, bishops, and princes of the blood, drew off the attention of every body from the public good, and from every political and ambitious view, by filling them with the dread of losing, and the thirst of gain. It was a great and extraordinary game of hazard, at which the citizens betted against each other. Earnest gamesters never lay aside their cards in order to disturb the government. It happened by a sort of delusion, whose springs

men was sent towards that kingdom, under the command of the duke of Berwick.

will for ever remain hidden from all but the most experienced and piercing eyes, that a system altogether chimerical, gave rise to a real commerce, and caused to flourish a-new the company of the Indies, which had before been established by the celebrated Colbert, and ruined by the wars. In a word, though the fortunes of many private persons were destroyed, the nation, in general, in a short time became more rich, and its trade more extensive. This system enlightened the minds of men in the same manner that civil wars whet their courage.

This was an epidemical disease, which soon spread from France to Holland and England: it is worthy the attention of posterity; for it was not the political interest of two or three princes that thus turned whole nations topsy-turvy. The people of their own accord ran headlong into this folly, which enriched some families, and reduced many more to beggary. A Scotchman, named John Law, whom we call John Lass, who had no other employment than that of a gamester and calculator, was obliged to fly from Great Britain on account of a murder: he had a long time before digested the plan of a company, which was to pay the debts of a state by bank-notes, and reimburse itself with the profits. This system was extremely complicated; but, under proper regulations, it might have been made of great use. It was an imitation of the English bank and India company. He proposed this establishment to the duke of Savoy Victor Amadeus, since first king of Sardinia, who answered, that he was not great enough to ruin himself.

He proposed it likewise to the comptroller general Des Marets; but that was at the time of an unfortunate war, by which all credit was annihilated; and credit was the basis of this system.

In fine, he found the regency of the duke of Orleans a juncture every way favourable; a debt of two thousand millions to pay, a peace which left the government at leisure, and a prince and people passionately fond of novelties.

He first of all established a bank in his own name, in the year 1716. This soon became a general office of the receipts of the kingdom. To this was joined the company of the Mississippi; a company from which the public was persuaded to hope for extraordinary advantages. The people being seduced by the allurements of hope, ran with the utmost eagerness to purchase the actions of this company and bank united. Wealth, which was before locked up by the distrustful, now began to circulate with profusion; the company's notes encreased this wealth two and even fourfold. In effect, France became extremely rich by the influence of credit. Luxury became known to men in every station of life; and it passed to the neighbours of France, who had a share in this commerce.

The bank was declared a royal bank in 1718. It undertook to manage the commerce of Senegal, and acquired the privilege of the old India company, founded by the celebrated Colbert, which had fallen since his time, and resigned its commerce to the traders of St. Malo. In fine, it took upon itself the general farms of the whole kingdom. Thus was all the wealth of the whole kingdom in the hands of Law, and the finances themselves depended upon a trading company.

As this company appeared to be established upon such great funds, its actions increased to more than twenty times their first value. The frequent variations in the price of these effects brought immense fortunes to obscure persons: Many in less than six months became more opulent than some sovereigns. Law, dazzled by his own system, and intoxicated by the public frenzy as well as his own, had made so many notes, that the imaginary value of actions amounted in 1719 to eighty times the money that could circulate in the kingdom. The government reimbursed all the tenants of the state by paper.

The regent was unable to govern a machine so immense and

complicated, whose rapid motion hurried him on, whether he would or not. The ancient financiers, and the wealthy bankers united, exhausted the royal bank by making considerable draughts upon it. Every body tried to change their notes for cash; but the disproportion was enormous. Credit sunk all of a sudden; the regent strove to revive it by edicts which entirely destroyed it. Nothing was then seen but paper; real misery began to succeed so much imaginary wealth. At this juncture the place of comptroller-general was conferred upon Law, exactly at a time when it was impossible for him to acquit himself of the duties required by it; it was in 1720, an epocha rendered remarkable by the subversion of all private fortunes, and of the revenues of the kingdom. He was seen soon after to become, by naturalization, a Frenchman of a Scotchman; a catholic of a protestant; of an adventurer, a lord possessed of one of the finest estates of the kingdom; and of a banker a minister of state. The disorder was risen to its highest pitch. The parliament of Paris made all the opposition in its power to these innovations, and was therefore banished to Pontoise. In fine, during the course of the same year, Law, loaded with the public execration, was obliged to fly from the country which he had turned topsy-turvy by attempting to enrich it.

The regent is charged in libels published at that time with having seized all the specie of the kingdom, that he might be in a condition to effect his ambitious designs; and it cannot be denied that he died seven millions in debt. Law was accused by the same authors of having sent the current coin of France into foreign countries for his own emolument: he lived for some time at London, being supported by the generosity of the marquis of Lassay, and died at Venice in circumstances just above indigence. Such revolutions are not the least useful objects which history offers to our consideration.

During this time the plague made terrible havock in

Provence: the war with Spain still continued: Bretagne was ripe for rebellion: conspiracies had been formed against the regent; yet notwithstanding all this he, with scarce any difficulty, succeeded in all he undertook, either at home or abroad. The kingdom was in a confusion, which occasioned universal dread; yet this was the reign of pleasure and voluptuousness.

After the system of Law had failed, it was necessary to reform the state; an estimation was made of the fortunes of all the citizens, a step no less extraordinary than the system itself: this was the greatest and most difficult operation of exchequer ever made in any nation.

It was begun about the close of the year 1721. It was contrived, digested, and conducted by four brothers, who till then never had any considerable share in public affairs, and who by their genius and industry were worthy of being intrusted with the revenues of the state. They erected a proper number of offices for masters of requests and other judges; they formed a certain and simple method, whereby to extricate affairs from the chaos wherein they were plunged; five hundred eleven thousand and five citizens, most of them fathers of families, carried their fortunes in paper to this tribunal. All these innumerable debts were cleared for about sixteen hundred and thirty-two numerary millions in ready cash, for which the state was accountable. Thus ended this extraordinary game of hazard, which an obscure stranger had caused the whole nation to play. After the demolishing of this vast edifice of Law, so boldly conceived, and which crushed its own architect, there still remained of its ruins an India company, which soon became the rival of those of London and Amsterdam.

The infatuation for venturing money upon the actions of a company, which had turned the heads of the French, soon after intoxicated the Dutch and English. Those who had examined the springs by which so many private persons in France had suddenly raised immense fortunes upon the credulity and misery of the public, introduced the same artifice and the same folly in Amsterdam, Rotterdam, and London: companies were established, and an imaginary commerce set on foot. Amsterdam was soon undeceived, Rotterdam was for some time reduced almost to ruin. London was full of confusion and tumult during the year 1720. This frenzy produced in France and England a prodigious number of bankruptcies, frauds, public impositions, and all that depravity of manners which is the natural result of a boundless avarice.

BIBLIOGRAPHY

I. MANUSCRIPTS

Adams, Gavin John. *The Lauriston Lecture: John Law of Lauriston.* From the original manuscript of the lecture delivered by Gavin John Adams at Lauriston Castle, Edinburgh, Scotland, 2011.

II. ARCHIVES

The Proceedings of the Old Bailey, 18 April 1694. Reference Number: t16940418-28.

III. PRINTED WORKS

Adams, Gavin John. *Letters to John Law.* Washington, D.C.: Newton Page, 2012.

Defoe, Daniel. *John Law and the Mississippi Scheme: An Anthology.* Edited by Gavin John Adams. Washington, D.C.: Newton Page, 2014.

Defoe, Daniel. *Robinson Crusoe.* London: W. Taylor, 1719.

Defoe, Daniel. *The Chimera, or, The French Way of Paying National Debts Laid Open*. London: T. Warner, 1720.

Defoe, Daniel. *The Chimera, or, The French Way of Paying National Debts Laid Open*. Edited by Gavin John Adams. Washington D.C.: Newton Page, 2014.

Gleeson, Janet. *The Moneymaker*. London: 1999.

Horace. *The Satires and Epistles of Horace*. Translated by Smith Palmer Bovie. Chicago: The University of Chicago Press, 2002.

Irving, Washington. *The Knickerbocker: Or, New York Monthly Magazine*, Volume 15. New York: 1840.

Irving, Washington. *Chronicles of Wolfert's Roost and Other Papers*. Leipzig: Bernhard Tauchnitz, 1855.

Law, John. *Money and Trade Considered, With a Proposal for Supplying the Nation with Money*. Edinburgh, 1705.

Law, John. *Money and Trade Considered, With a Proposal for Supplying the Nation with Money*. Edited by Gavin John Adams. Washington D.C.: Newton Page, 2013.

Law, John. *The Present State of the French Revenues and Trade, and of the Controversy betwixt the Parliament of Paris, and Mr. Law*. Edited by Gavin John Adams. Washington D.C.: Newton Page, 2015.

Mackay, Charles. *Memoirs of Extraordinary Popular Delusions and the Madness of Crowds*. London: Richard Bentley, 1841.

Marshall, Alfred. *Money, Credit and Commerce,* London: Macmillan and Company, 1923

Marx, Karl. *Das Capital,* Vol III. Hamburg: Otto Meissner, 1894.

Murphy, Antoin. John Law. Oxford: Clarendon Press, 1996.

Schumpeter, Joseph. *History of Economic Analysis.* New York: Oxford University Press, 1954.

Smith, Adam. *An Inquiry into the Nature and Causes of the Wealth of Nations.* London: W. Strahan and T. Cadell, 1776.

Smith, Adam. *Lectures on Justice, Police, Revenue and Arms.* Oxford: The Clarendon Press, 1896.

Stoker, Bram. *Famous Imposters.* New York: Sturgis & Walton Company, 1910.

Voltaire. *The Works of M. de Voltaire.* London: J. Newbery, R. Baldwin, W. Johnston, S. Crowder, T. Davies, J. Coote, G. Kearsley, and B. Collins, 1761.

ALSO AVAILABLE FROM NEWTON PAGE

The Financier Law

His Scheme and Times: A Graphic Description of the Origin, Maturity and Wreck of the Mississippi Scheme

André Cochut

ISBN-13: 978-1934619049

A richly contextual narrative of the life of John Law, a charismatic Scottish economist and murderer and who would escape execution and use his seemingly effortless financial genius to rise from obscurity to become the most powerful member of the French court, the controller of the French economy, and the richest man the modern world had ever seen.

ALSO AVAILABLE FROM NEWTON PAGE

The Memoirs Life and Character of the Great Mr. Law and his Brother at Paris

Down to this Present Year 1721, with an Accurate and Particular Account of the Establishment of the Missisippi Company in France, the rise and fall of it's Stock, and all the Subtle artifices used to support the National Credit of that Kingdom, by the Pernicious Project of Paper-Credit.

Mr. Gray

ISBN-13: 978-1-934619094

As a writer employed by Law in his Parisian *comptoir* during the period in which he was the Controller General of France, Gray provides a first-hand account of many aspects of the rise and fall of both Law and his Mississippi Scheme. An important pamphlet which has been used as source material for all biographies of John Law.

ALSO AVAILABLE FROM NEWTON PAGE

A Full and Impartial Account of the Company of Mississippi:

Otherwise Call'd the French East India Company, Projected and Settled by Mr. Law

Anon

ISBN-13: 978-1-934619124

First published as a propagandist pamphlet (in both French and English) in 1720, it was not really an 'impartial account' at all, as it was commissioned, written and published primarily to both reassure existing investors, and encourage potential investors, of the advantages to be gained by becoming a shareholder in John Law's Mississippi Company.

Made in the USA
Monee, IL
08 November 2026

67383846R00125